CHAMPIONSHIP

OMAHA

HIGH-LOW · POT-LIMIT · LIMIT

"Tom and T.J. have put together a 'super system' for winning at Omaha."

Doyle "Texas Dolly" Brunson, two-time World Champion of Poker; author of *Super System* and *Super System 2*

"In this book, you can rope in some mighty powerful advice on winning at Omaha that might just help you round up a championship or two for yourself."

-Byron "Cowboy" Wolford, 1991 Limit Hold'em World Champion

CHAMPIONSHIP

OMAHA

HIGH-LOW · POT-LIMIT · LIMIT

T.J. CLOUTIER & TOM McEVOY

CARDOZA PUBLISHING

Cardoza Publishing is the foremost gaming publisher in the world with a library of more than 200 up-to-date and easy-to-read books and strategies. These authoritative works are written by the top experts in their fields and with more than 10,000,000 books in print, represent the most popular gaming books anywhere.

THIRD EDITION

First Printing   October 2009

Copyright© 1999, 2005, 2009 by T.J. Cloutier, Tom McEvoy
& Dana Smith
All Rights Reserved

ISBN 13: 978-1-5804-2259-8
ISBN 10: 1-58042-259-4

Library of Congress Control Number: 2008940744

ABOUT THE AUTHORS

T.J. Cloutier was inducted into the Poker Hall of Fame in 2006. He won the Player of the Year award in 1998 and 2002, and is considered to be one of the best tournament players in the world. Cloutier has won six World Series of Poker bracelets, and has appeared at the final table of the WSOP Main Event a remarkable four times, placing second in 1985 and in 2000. Overall, he has won more titles in no-limit and pot-limit hold'em than any other tournament player in the history of poker. Cloutier is the author of *How to Win the Championship*, and the co-author (with Tom McEvoy) of *Championship No-Limit & Pot-Limit Hold'em*, *Championship Omaha*, *Championship Hold'em* and *Championship Tournament Practice Hands*.

Tom McEvoy, the "Champion of Champions" has one of the most storied tournament careers of any poker player in history. In addition to winning four WSOP gold bracelets including the main event championship in 1983, McEvoy won the inaugural Champion of Champions tournament at the 2009 World Series of Poker in competition against the other living winners of the World Championship of Poker. He also won the 2005 Professional Poker Tour tournament sponsored by the World Poker Tour—an exclusive invitation-only event featuring the best players in the world—becoming the first player ever to win a PPT championship *and* a WSOP main event championship. A pioneer in improving conditions for poker players by sponsoring the nonsmoking movement in poker venues, McEvoy is the author and co-author of more than twelve other titles.

TABLE OF CONTENTS

2. OMAHA HIGH-LOW 35

4. LIMIT OMAHA HIGH   131

TABLE OF CONTENTS

6. POT-LIMIT & LIMIT HIGH HANDS IN ACTION   187

7. THE TOURNAMENT TRAIL: TACTICS AND TALES   219

TABLE OF CONTENTS

FOREWORD

by Bob Ciaffone

World-Class Poker Player &
Author of *Improve Your Poker*

I have known Tom McEvoy and T.J. Cloutier for many years and am well acquainted with their poker careers. I can certainly vouch for the fact that they have relied on playing poker as the main source of their income for the entire time that I have known them and that they have achieved high stature in the poker world.

Tom won the title of World Champion at the 1983 World Series of Poker. Although he plays in both money games and tournaments, he is best known as a tournament competitor. Tom is one of the country's most experienced and knowledgeable poker tournament competitors, and he has written extensively on that subject.

Recently, he joined forces with T.J. in his writing efforts, and this is the second book produced by that alliance. Over the last ten years, T.J. has established himself as the most successful tournament player in poker, having won the premier event of major poker tournaments, the grand finale no-limit hold'em competition, which has the largest buy-in amount of any event.

We are all fortunate that both Tom and T.J., two of the best poker players in the world, have put their thoughts on paper for our benefit. Their goal is to help you, the Omaha player, improve your game. In the following pages, they'll cover tournament play, pot-limit Omaha high, limit Omaha high, limit Omaha eight-or-better, and even low-stakes play.

The authors' tone is conversational, so I am sure that you will be entertained as well as educated.

I have to admit that I've improved my own game by copying a number of plays that I have seen T.J. put on his opponents over the years. Of course, reasonable men may differ in the fine tuning they wish to apply to their poker game, but I can certainly vouch for the fact that T.J. and Tom have enjoyed great success with the ideas they'll pass on to you in this book. Anyone can benefit from the top-flight professional advice they dispense.

INTRODUCTION
Tom McEvoy

Once again I've had the pleasure of collaborating with T.J. Cloutier, my friend and world-class poker player, on a poker book. Our first book, *Championship No-Limit and Pot-Limit Hold'em*, was successful beyond imagination. It has enjoyed steadily increasing demand for the past few years, not only from gambling bookstores across the nation but from mainstream international booksellers as well.

Our success story with the hold'em book has been so gratifying that we have decided to write *Championship Omaha* on all three types of Omaha, games for which we've won four World Series of Poker bracelets between us. In this book T.J. and I share some of the strategies we've used to get to the winners' circle in Omaha cash games and tournaments. Our goal is to show you how to get there too.

In the opening chapter we discuss several basic principles of winning play at any type of Omaha game. Particularly important is the concept that you should always play four cards that work together and avoid hands with a *dangler*, a card that doesn't work with your other three cards. We'll expand on this concept throughout the strategy chapters on Omaha high-low, pot-limit Omaha, and limit Omaha high.

Shane Smith described Omaha high-low as a game that was invented by a sadist and is played by masochists. T.J., who won the Omaha high-low title at the World Series in 1994, takes the lead in the high-low chapter, where he stresses the importance of hand value and drawing to the nuts.

Pot-limit Omaha is one of the most exciting, big-bet games in poker. At the World Series of Poker in 1998, T.J. overcame terrific opposition at the final table of the pot-limit Omaha event to emerge victorious over such world-class players as Doyle Brunson and Erik Seidel. In the pot-limit chapter, he explains how to win the money in this roller-coaster game that is a favorite of many of the world's highest-stakes players.

Since I won the championship in limit Omaha high in 1992, I take the lead in the Omaha high chapter, and T.J. adds his commentary. In this chapter we explain how the limit game differs from the pot-limit version, and why limit Omaha high is not only one of the most volatile games in poker but one of the most exciting as well.

In Chapter 5, we present twenty-two Omaha hands and describe how T.J. and I play them in ring games and tournaments. We have included cash game strategy and tournament tips in each of the game chapters, with some follow-up advice on playing tournaments in Chapter 6.

No book authored by T.J. would be complete without a few of his famous road stories, which you'll find in Chapter 7, followed by a glossary of poker terms used in this book. After all, not everyone will understand what T.J. means when he says, "He was playing a dangler, and when the board ragged off on the end, he was a gone goose."

Our best efforts have gone into the writing of *Championship Omaha,* and we sincerely hope that you get as much out of it as we have put into it. Study the strategies in this book, and I'm sure that T.J. and I will be seeing you in the winner's circle.

A TRIBUTE TO BENNY

T.J. Cloutier

I'll never forget Benny Binion's birthday party not long before he died. It was held at Cowboy's in Fort Worth, Texas, a great big Western place with food and drink—it even has a little rodeo arena and a big dance hall where all the best country bands play.

People came from all over the world to pay tribute to Benny. He hadn't been able to go back to Texas for all those years because he'd had outstanding charges against him or something like that, but he finally got them quashed. Everybody who's anybody showed up—Bobby Baldwin, Doyle Brunson—they all were there. Cowboy's is enormous and it was packed for this tribute to Benny. His family threw the party, and Doyle might have had something to do with it, too, since they were close friends. Benny's former bodyguard, R. D. Matthews (everybody called him "Patch"), probably was in on the party also.

Benny was all decked out for his birthday bash. He always wore Western suits and a beige 20-X Stetson, the best you can buy. He was the type of guy that, if you caught him on a good day—say you got broke and he knew you, and he knew that you gambled in his joint—you could go to him and get a couple of thousand dollars without putting up any security. He'd just flip it to you and say, "Pay it when you can, son." Jack Binion was the same way.

It's funny how we're all connected a little bit. Just after he'd had an aneurysm, Lyle Berman was playing in a tournament at the Horseshoe and fell over in his chair. I took Lyle to the hospital and while we were there, I heard that Benny was in the hospital, too, so I went up to see him. I've always been thankful that I was able to see him that night, the night before he died. One of his nephews was sitting beside his bed and although Benny couldn't recognize me, at least I could say good-bye to him.

Benny left a legacy to the world of poker. By starting the World Series of Poker, he essentially reversed poker's questionable reputation and made it legitimate in the eyes of non-poker players by putting it into casinos. Amarillo Slim had a lot to do with that, too. For all his flamboyance and the way he talks on TV and all that stuff, Slim has done a lot for poker. But mainly it was Benny; the World Series of Poker is what started it all, and we owe a big debt of gratitude to him for that.

How do you replace a guy like Benny? You don't.

What poker players can do now to improve the reputation of poker is to stop acting like idiots, quit throwing cards and getting up and stomping around the poker table when they take a beat. If they don't clean up their act, poker will end up right back where it started, in the backroom, because people aren't going to continue putting up with that kind of stuff. Benny helped bring it out of the backrooms, and we owe it to him to preserve his legacy.

I mean, in the old days if somebody asked you what you did for a living, if you were a poker player you told them that you were in investments, right? Or I do this, or I do that. Nowadays if they ask you what you do for a living, you can just say, "I play poker." That's a big difference.

And we owe it all to Benny.

Though both T.J. and Tom worked together on all sections of the book, the lead author's name appears under the title of each chapter. The "I" used in these chapters refers to the lead author.

HOW TO WIN AT OMAHA

HOW TO WIN AT OMAHA

T.J. Cloutier

Our goal in this book is to give you the best advice possible so that you can become a consistent winner at any form of Omaha. Or as our motto for this series of books goes, "Let the champions lead you to the winners circle."

First, understand that all forms of Omaha are driven by hand value. That is, the starting value of your hand is paramount to your position at the table. Position is far less important in Omaha than it is in limit or pot-limit hold'em.

Keeping this underlying principle in mind, let's look at nine things you must do to become a winner at any form of Omaha.

NINE PRINCIPLES FOR WINNING AT OMAHA

1. Understand the Value of Your Hand

In no other form of poker is hand value as important as it is in Omaha. The primary factor in determining the value of your hand is having four related cards that work together in some way.

On the flop you should have either the best hand possible or a draw to it to justify continuing with the hand. If you have a drawing hand, you need to have a draw that will win the pot if you make it; that is, not the second-best draw, the very best draw. When you draw for flushes, draw for the nut flush. When you draw for straights, draw for the nut straight. In other words, you should only be drawing to the nuts.

2. Have the Best Draw with Backup

When you have a drawing hand, you should have a backup to your draw, a secondary draw. For example, in Omaha high-low you might flop top set and also have a low draw or a three-flush for backup. In Omaha high, you might flop the top set or second set, plus a draw to the nut flush or nut straight to go with it. Your backup draws give you a lot more ways to make the hand stand up than if you have only one draw. This concept is important in ring games and is especially important in tournaments.

Let's say that you're playing a pot-limit Omaha tournament and make a set on the flop with no straight or flush possibilities in your hand—that is, you have no backup draw. If either a flush or straight card comes on fourth street, are you going to call a big bet to try to pair the board on the end? You really have to be careful in these situations in tournaments, where having a backup draw is so important to your survival.

3. Avoid Playing Hands with Danglers

A lot of people play hands that I call "three cards with a dangler." Say that you have K-Q-J-2. Obviously, the deuce doesn't fit with anything else—it's a dangler. But you see a lot of people playing this type of hand, even a lot of good players in big games. They know that the three high cards can become straights, big full houses, or high sets, so they discount the value of having a fourth connecting card. As for me, I can't do that. I won't play a dangler hand like K-Q-J-2, even if the king happens to be suited, because you never have the nut flush draw with it.

You want four cards that interact with each other in some fashion.

The times when you might consider playing a three-card hand usually are in unraised pots, late position (on or next to the button), and when three of your cards are fairly strong. You virtually never play one from up front unless you happen to be in the big or small blind.

A lot of people play a lot of hands, and they don't always have four cards that interact. They slip in with three-card hands.

And a lot of times they slip right out of the game busted.

4. Get to Know Your Opponents

As in every other form of poker, you have to get to know the players in your Omaha game. Who will raise before the flop with bare aces unsuited in Omaha high? Who won't? Who will only raise with aces double-suited? Who will only raise with A-K-Q-J double-suited? In Omaha high-low, who will only raise with A-A-2-3?

You must find out who those players are as quickly as possible.

Tom was playing in a $20/$40 Omaha high-low game with a kill pot. He put in a $20 bet on the button. Fred, who would never get out of line, raises from the big blind and gets called by one other player. Tom knew that Fred had one of the following three hands: an A-2 with two little cards working, an A-2 with a big pair, or aces with two face cards. Tom had a 10-9-7-6 with $20 already in the pot and knew exactly where Fred is at, although the third player's hand was a bit of a mystery. So, Tom decides to call $20 more.

The flop comes J-8-8, three different suits.

TOM   **FRED**   **THIRD PLAYER**

FLOP

Fred comes out betting and the third player folds. You know what Tom does? He raises. Fred thinks about it for a few seconds and mucks his hand, showing it to Tom first. He had A-2-Q-Q with one suit.

Recently, I lost money in a $40/$80 game, but I learned something about a player that I hadn't played with before. Every time he had a hand, he check-raised on the flop. Not once did he ever lead.

What does this tell me?

I'm never going to bet any marginal hands on the flop when this man is in the pot. If I bet when he's in the pot with me, I'm going to be sure I have the goods. In the long run, that knowledge will save me a lot of money. In any game you play, no matter what the limits, you have to learn the playing styles of your opponents and learn them well.

Suppose the flop comes K-Q-4 and you have a king and queen in your hand. You bet and get called in a couple of spots. On fifth street comes a jack. You check and your opponent bets. If you've been watching the game and you know how he plays, you might say to yourself, "I know he didn't make a straight. I've got this man tied in this hand," so you make the call. But if you haven't been watching how he plays, you might automatically give him credit for the straight and lay down your hand.

There are situations where you have to call if you know the type of player who's making the bet. If for instance, you know that your opponent is a good enough player to make the bet with kings and queens in order to represent the straight when there's a K-Q-J on the board, and if he knows that you're a good enough player to throw the hand away, you have to call.

Watch your opponents' betting habits. Note the cards they show down at the end. Get a feel for their comfort level in the game. Will they protect their blinds? Are they passive or aggressive? Who can you run over, and who should you avoid?

Knowing these things about your opponents, coupled with good hand selection, will lead you to the winners' circle time after time, tournament after tournament.

5. Think Ahead of the Play

In bridge, you have to think three or four tricks ahead in the play. In football, you have to plan several plays ahead of the snap. You have to learn to play poker in the same way. It should always be in your mind that if this card comes, you can do this, and if that card comes, you can do that; and if the rest of them come, you can't do anything. That way, when the cards come on the flop, you can move right away. You're always playing ahead of yourself.

Right after the flop, you should know how you're going to play the entire hand depending on what slips off the deck after the flop.

When you get to the point that you see the big picture before it fully develops, you are in the flow of the game and your results will improve dramatically.

6. Read the Board Correctly

Deciding how your cards mesh with the cards on the flop, turn and river is a skill that you absolutely must develop to be successful at Omaha. On the surface, it sounds easy, but fitting two of your hole cards to three board cards complicates matters, especially for Texas hold'em players who are beginners at Omaha.

Novice players seem to get mixed up most often when a set comes on the board. They don't have a pair in their hand but they have an ace, and there's an ace on the board. They forget that they have to play two cards from their hand and that if they don't have a pair in their hand, they don't have a full house. Of all the mistakes I've seen people make in Omaha, that is the biggest one.

A big mistake that Omaha high-low players make is not reading their hand correctly when they get counterfeited for low. A player might have an A-2-4-7 in his hand, for example, and A-5-8 comes on the board. Since the ace is showing on the board, he thinks he's been counterfeited, whereas his 2-4 give him the second-best low possible. As simple a mistake as this is, it is very common.

If you have problems reading the board, try practicing at home by dealing several different flops for the same hand.

7. Play Decision Hands Carefully

Great hands play themselves, and terrible hands play themselves. It is how you play the in-between hands that can make you or break you in poker. You've heard about the farmer who lost three farms by drawing to inside straights and missing?

Then he lost the fourth farm when he drew to one and hit it. The same adage applies in Omaha.

You must have enough skill and discipline to draw to only the nuts and be able to recognize when your draw is less than the nuts but is still the best draw. Knowing when that king-high flush draw is the best flush draw out there and that if you hit it, maybe a queen-high flush draw will pay you off—that takes great skill. As does knowing when you have the best hand with two pair and forcing people out of the pot to protect it. Making the right decisions in these situations makes your long-term profit.

Decision hands are the bread and butter hands of the pros. Making the right decisions in these situations is what separates the winning pros from the wannabes. Anybody can play powerful hands or powerful flops and win pots. And most players can recognize trash hands and get away from them cheaply.

It is the decisions that you make about all of the in-between hands that separate the men from the boys, and the women from the girls, in the poker world. And that's where you win or lose most of your money. For example, what do you do when you flop top two pair, which can be a very marginal holding in Omaha? Winning players know when the hand is good, when to push it to increase its chances of holding up, and when to get loose from it.

You can have a great winning session just by having the deck hit you in the face, or a losing session when you don't catch any cards at all. And you can lose when you have good cards but run into someone with better cards, like when you flop set over set and you have the worst set; when you have all your money in on a set or top two pair and someone hits a flush at the river and takes you off; or when you have the flush and someone fills on the end.

This is why losing players sometimes have winning sessions against very strong professional-level players. But that's what keeps the lesser-skilled players coming back. Omaha is a volatile game, which means that weak players can play a lot of cards and might catch enough cards or backdoor enough hands on a given day to have a very successful individual winning session. But loose play almost guarantees long-term disastrous results, losing results.

8. Don't Go on Tilt

Let me tell you a story about one of the worst beats I've seen happen in a tournament. In a no-limit hold'em championship event at a big tournament some years ago, John Bonetti flopped a set of jacks and Milt Meyers flopped a set of fives. They got all their money in on the flop. On the river Meyers caught a one-outer, the case 5, to knock Bonetti out of the tournament.

It's pretty easy for players to go on tilt when things like this happen to them. Everybody who has ever played poker has gone on tilt at some time or other. The idea is to learn from it—if you've gone on tilt ten times, don't make it eleven.

Getting up and walking away when you're losing more than you're comfortable with in a poker game should be the easiest thing in the world to do. I can almost count on one hand the times that I've gone off for a big number in a game. When I say a big number, I mean something like when you buy in for $5,000 and lose it, then put up another $5,000 and lose that. That's when you just have to say, "It's not my day, they'll be playing again tomorrow," and walk away.

I've always set a loss limit. I know that some experts say that, whether you're winning or losing, you should stay in a game if you're playing well and the game's good. My theory is that there's almost always a game the next day. I play well enough that I can overcome a $10,000 loss, but what if I get

$30,000 into a game and the game the next day isn't going to be as big? Sometimes, big games are random occurrences—they start off as little games and build into big ones. So, if I take a $30,000 loss I might have to wait two months before I can get into a game where I can get that money back.

Have I worked for two months playing smaller games to earn $30,000 only to blow it in one game? That just does not make sense, yet people do it all the time.

9. Keep a Positive Attitude and Use Good Instincts

It doesn't matter what the game is, you should have a good attitude when you sit down to play in a poker game. Always try to play your best. If you have an inclination to do something that you know you shouldn't do, go with your instincts and don't do it.

The things we know are based on what we've learned over the years. Your first instinct is going to be right a high percentage of the time. But if you sit there like a goose and construct a way that you could possibly have the best hand by putting your opponents on hands that you can beat, you're a fool. You have no chance to win at poker.

Keep your attitude positive and your instincts active. That way, you'll always have the edge.

MOVING FORWARD

Now that we've covered a few general principles of winning at Omaha, Tom and I will discuss specific pointers on how to win at each type of Omaha. We have included both cash game strategies and tournament techniques in the chapters on Omaha high-low, pot-limit Omaha, and limit Omaha high. Then we will show you several practice hands that regularly come up in

Omaha and give you our opinions on how to profitably play them in all three versions of Omaha.

OMAHA HIGH-LOW

OMAHA HIGH-LOW

T.J. Cloutier

People think of Omaha high-low as a relatively new game, but we were playing it in Texas in the '70s so it's been around a lot longer than most people realize. It's a game that pulls in weak players like no other. A lot of today's casino players have no idea about which hands to play or the odds of scooping a pot. That's one reason why there are so many multiway pots in the low-limit games.

To start with, let's examine four important concepts in Omaha high-low.

FOUR IMPORTANT OMAHA HIGH-LOW CONCEPTS

1. Your Four Cards Must Work Together

Omaha high-low is a hand-value driven game. Just like other four-card hold'em games, you should not be entering pots unless all four of your cards work together in some way. You usually don't want to play a hand with three good cards and a dangler in it because that dangler—the one card that doesn't fit in with the rest of them—can put you in a world of misery. Remember the word dangler because you'll be seeing it a lot in this book.

2. Omaha High-Low is a Two-Tiered Game

Omaha high-low is a two-tiered game: You play big cards or you play little cards. You do not play middle hands. You play Omaha high-low as though you were playing with a stripped deck, as though the sevens, eights, and nines aren't in the deck. Repeat to yourself, "I cannot win playing sevens, eights and nines in this game."

You might win a few pots with middle hands, but you'll get eaten alive in the long run. Big hands are big pairs with connectors and **big rundowns**—connecting high cards—and little hands are those with **little rundowns** that include an ace. A pair of aces with a deuce-trey is both big and little. You like this hand because you usually can't get counterfeited for low with it. You also like two aces with a deuce and some other low card. These are the types of hands to play.

Any time you're playing Omaha high-low, you want to have an ace in your hand. The middle cards have a lot of value in Omaha high but almost no value in Omaha high-low. The main difference between the hands that you play in Omaha high and pot-limit Omaha and the ones you play in Omaha high-low is that you play the middle cards in the high games, but you don't play them in high-low.

3. Raising is Seldom Correct Before the Flop

Hare some basic betting tips that will help you play Omaha high-low more profitably. Never be overly aggressive unless you have a very strong hand on the flop. Raising at one of the two-bet levels is worth a lot more to you than at the single-bet levels. So, make your moves later in the play, at the double-bet level. (I'll explain these concepts in greater detail throughout the chapter.)

"Hal Kant gave me a piece of strong advice for Omaha high-low," Tom says. "When you have four premium low cards in your hand, such as A-2-4-5, you should not bring it in for a raise because you want as many players as possible to come into the pot with you. They won't be expecting you to have that strong a hand in an unraised pot."

In Omaha high-low, you're going to get played with most of the time because it's a limit-structure game, which means there will usually be a lot of players in every pot. When you raise before the flop, you're tipping the strength of your hand.

I'm not saying that you never raise before the flop in Omaha high-low: In fact, I probably raise more before the flop in Omaha high-low, where raising costs only one unit, than I ever would in pot-limit Omaha. In Omaha high-low, if you don't flop to your hand, you can get away from it anyway, so it's cheap.

The purpose of raising in Omaha high-low is to build the pot, not to limit the field. It's difficult to eliminate anybody because if someone is going to play the hand, he'll call at least one raise. When you come in with premium cards, you're hoping to induce somebody with a hand such as K-Q-2-3 to play with you. By the way, as far as I'm concerned, a K-Q-2-3 is just sucker bait. You have no nut-flush draws and if there's any action before the flop, you know that the aces are gone so it's less likely that you'll catch your key card, an ace.

4. Look for the Right Situation

Some marginal hands can be played in exactly the right situations, even in tournaments. For example, suppose only one guy has called the pot in Omaha high-low and you're around back with 2-3-4-5, and you don't think you'll get raised. This isn't a super-strong hand, but in this situation you can play it. You're hoping to catch an ace or make a straight to win the high end, or you might even have the best low against only one player. At least you know that an ace probably is available because there's been no action before the flop.

Since it costs you just one limit bet, you can call. Then if an ace and another low card come on the flop, you're in hog heaven. If you catch the ace and another little card that pairs one of yours, you have a pair, yes, but you have the wheel draw and a low going for you with the chance for a scooper.

However, if three or four people have come into the pot in front of you, that 2-3-4-5 is nothing. It's a piece of cheese because the aces are already busy. Suppose the flop comes with 8-6-3. You have a straight draw, yes, but with the aces out, you won't have the nut low unless an ace hits the board. Also, any straight that you make won't be the nuts, so you can get into further trouble. This is *el trappo cigarus*—it'll come rock-rock and you'll lose all your money.

You have to think about all these things when you're playing Omaha high-low, especially in a multiway pot in late position when it looks like the aces are gone. If four other players are in the pot with you, you can just about bank on two of the aces being busy.

STARTING HANDS

One reason that Omaha high-low is so popular these days is that so many people don't know what hands to play and the good players take advantage of them. The good players will beat these bad players to death. If the flop comes K-9-3 and the bad player has four little cards in his hand, he'll stay in to see fourth street. Almost invariably fourth street gives him another low card, which justifies calling another bet. Then it rags on the end and he's a gone goose for all the money he's put in the pot. He will remember the one time he made a hand like that and forget the ten times he lost to it. Tom calls this "selective memory."

The Low Starting Hands

The best hand is A-A-2-3 double-suited, followed by A-A-2-3 with one suit and A-A-2-3 with no suit. After these hands come A-A-2-4 and A-A-2-5. Then an A-2-3-4, A-2-3-5. A-2-3-K or A-2-3-Q suited are great hands, too. The really good players always have the ace suited when they're playing any decent-sized pot.

Best Low Starting Omaha Hands

A-A-2-3 double-suited
A-A-2-3 with one suit
A-A-2-3 with no suit
A-A-2-4
A-A-2-5
A-2-3-4
A-2-3-5

These low hands rate higher than hands like A-A-K-Q or other premium high hands. A hand such as A-2-K-Q is good, but it can get counterfeited very easily. You should always have a third low card to help protect you from getting counterfeited.

Remember that a hand like A-2-3-4 will only cost you the original bet or raise before the flop because if the flop comes with high cards, your A-2-3-4 is easy to get away from. Plus, it cannot get counterfeited for low unless you make four pair—and I've had that happen, too.

But hands like A-2-3-K or A-2-4-Q are harder to get away from and with certain types of flops, you can really get involved with them.

For example, suppose you have:

YOU

The flop comes:

FLOP

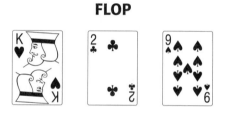

Now you have top and bottom pair and you'll have a nut-low draw if a little card comes on the turn. Things are looking good so you continue with the hand. But say the turn and river come 8♦ 9♠, 10♠ 10♦, or J♥ 10♥. Then what do you have? You're involved in the hand at this point because of your two pair on the flop and the nut-low draw you picked up on the turn, but on the end you have nothing!

Don't Chase a Low When the Flop Comes with Two High Cards

Weak players with good hands like A-2-3-4 will see the flop come with K-J-5 and call the first bet, trying to catch a low card. They get involved with the pot, maybe catch another low card on the turn, and then see another high card come or the board pair on the end, and wind up with nothing. That's the difference between a good player and a bad one. When a good player has a low hand, he will seldom chase unless at least two low cards come on the flop.

WEAK PLAYER WILL CHASE HERE

FLOP

Raising Before the Flop with Low Hands

You have to start with your premium low hands but you also must be careful with them. Ace-deuce alone is not a raising hand. A lot of players who get those premium low starting hands, such as A-2-3-4, in early position like to raise with them rather than just call in order to disguise the strength of their hands and entice weaker hands to come in after them. Rather than raise with premium low hands, you should wait to make your profit on the later streets. Instead, you usually should limp with them.

In Omaha high-low, there are very few occasions when you should raise from early position before the flop. Even if you have A-A-2-3 double-suited, I don't believe that you should raise the pot in most games. Of course, in a loose, ram-and-jam game where everybody's raising with everything, you can raise with this hand because the chances are good that you will get called in several spots. Usually, however, you don't want to tip your hand. You want to disguise its strength because you want a lot of other players to call, and you know that a raise might scare off four or five players who normally would have played. You want them in the pot because if you get a good flop to your hand, you can really make some money with it.

However if you're sitting around back and a couple of people already have come into the pot, that's a different story. If you have A-2-3-4 with the ace suited, you should raise the pot before the flop. If the players in front of you have called one bet, the chances are good that they will call the raise as well.

A player once asked me, "In a hold'em game, what if you had two aces, the pot was raised in first position, and there were tens, jacks, and queens? Would you play the hand?"

In a New York minute! In hold'em, there's no action that can keep me from playing or raising with two aces before the flop. Laying it down would be foolish.

But in Omaha high-low, I wouldn't ordinarily raise from up front with an A-A-2-3. From around back, I don't care what the action has been in front of me—even if it's been raised and reraised—I would put in another reraise with an A-A-2-3. If you are in late position with the best hand that you can possibly get before the flop, why wouldn't you raise with it?

However, if you have an A-2-8-9, why get heavily involved? Just to get a miracle flop? Say the flop comes 5-6-7 and now you have the nut low and the nut high, but how many times will that happen compared to the number of times the hand costs you money?

Low Hands Should Have an A-2 or A-3 and a Third Low Card

Remember that you always want a hand with an A-2 or an A-3 in it and at least one other low card. Anytime you can get an A-2 with two other low cards, that's fabulous. Even if you have A-2-6-8, you're going to play the hand. Actually, having the 2-6 to go along with your ace is stronger than you might think. You'll need a 3-4-5 on the board to make the wheel and thanks to the 6, you'll also have the 6-high straight.

The High Rundown Hands

You should only play big cards when you have hands like K-Q-J-10 and A-K-Q-J, or a big pair with connectors such as A-A-K-Q and K-K-Q-J—and you always want at least one suit. You should never play a hand with a dangler, such as Q-J-10-5 or K-J-10-3. That 5 and that 3 are classic examples of danglers.

High Hands Should Have Cards that Can Make an Ace-High Straight

When you play four high or semi-high straight cards, you always want to have two cards that can make a straight to the ace, so at the very least you need to have a J-10 in the hand. If you have a Q-J-10-8, for example, you have a shot at the high if an ace and any other high card come on the board. And you have a shot at getting some action on the hand because when an ace comes on the flop, somebody usually will have low cards to go with it or will make a pair of aces. The key is that when you play any four straight cards, you always want some part of the rundown to connect with an ace.

HIGH RUNDOWN THAT CAN CONNECT WITH ACE

Q-J-10-8 isn't necessarily a hand that I recommend playing, but if you're in late position and the pot is multiway, your opponents are usually going to have the low cards. As long as your cards can connect with an ace, you're in position to win either the high end or possibly scoop the whole pot if an ace comes on the board and a third low card doesn't come. You want the ace on the board because without it you're not going to get any action on the hand.

If you're in late position and there has been a lot of preflop action, you can be pretty sure that two or three aces are out. But if just one ace pops up on the flop, you can probably assume that at least one of your opponents has made a pair of aces, two pair or a low draw, and you will have a pretty good shot at scooping with a high straight.

Aces Are Usually Out When Preflop Action is Heavy

A lot of people play hands with any ace-deuce and random cards. If an ace comes on the flop—giving you two pair, for example—you might go from playing a low hand to playing a high hand. But if the flop comes with an ace and one other high card that connects, it might ruin your hand. You're not going to draw at a middle buster, or inside straight, in this situation; that would be ridiculous.

For example, say the flop comes A-10-4, and you have the Q-J-10-8.

YOU

FLOP

You're not going to draw for a king. But if it comes A-K-4, you have a good chance to scoop the pot if you catch a queen, jack, or 10.

But keep in mind that most pots that are scooped are not won by a hand that is going both ways. They're usually won by either a high hand or a wheel. Obviously, you would prefer having an ace in your high rundown hand. If an ace hits the board along with another big card, you'll have the wrap. Then you play the hand as though you are playing Omaha high and hope the little cards don't come, allowing you to scoop the pot.

Having a hand with a big pair and connecting high cards can be important, too. You might flop trips to it, and often they will be the top set. You don't want to flop middle or bottom trips because you might get tied into the pot and end up losing to someone with higher trips.

In a high hand other than the rundowns headed by an ace or king, I want to have a big pair, but I don't want them to be jacks. Two aces, kings, or queens with connecting big cards are fine and I'll play them, but two jacks are bad because if someone flops a bigger set than you, you're in trouble. This is why I consider K-Q-J-J to be a very marginal high hand in Omaha high-low. It looks pretty with all that color in it, but it could turn into a big trap for you if the flop comes with something like K-J-4 and there's a lot of action. Somebody could have the wrap going and somebody else could have three kings, so you're an underdog. Your only out may be the case jack!

The Big-Pair Hands

I'm not too enthralled with hands that have two big pair in them. Say that you have K-K-9-9. You almost have to flop a set to continue past the flop, and who says a set will win? And how many other hands can you make with two big pair in your hand?

BIG PAIR HAND

At the World Series of Poker you won't find many players who come in with those hands, although in the lower buy-in tournaments (up to $200), many players will play them. They don't really know how to play well, but get in cheap and want to play—they want to get action. And players like this are going to destroy a lot of good players. They have no chance of winning the tournament themselves, but they sometimes knock out serious contenders. You can't let it get you down when somebody knocks you out of a tournament with a hand they shouldn't have played. Without these players, nobody would win any money, so sometimes you just have to take your medicine.

Aces and Spaces

Aces with no connecting cards, or with **spaces**, are one-way hands. Suppose you have an A-A-9-6 with no suits and there's a raise in front of you. If an ace doesn't come on the flop, you'll probably only win with this hand if the board comes with a pair, such as tens, giving you aces-up. And even then, you'll only win as long as none of your opponents make a set of tens or a full. Always assume that at least one of your opponents is playing those low cards that can make straights and scoop the pot. Given that, you should realize that A-6 is not a good low draw!

People with just average skills will usually play any two aces but folding is the correct thing to do, especially in a tournament. However, suppose you're in a situation where you know you'll be playing heads-up against a late-position maniac who has raised in front of you. If you decide to play the hand in this situation, then you have to reraise. Otherwise, fold the hand. Once a maniac has put in one raise, he's usually going to go for a second.

Of course, anybody, even a maniac, can pick up a real hand, so I wouldn't raise with this hand. Let me give you an example: In a hold'em tournament, I had $2,500 in chips. I never put in all my chips with a hand like two queens, but I had played with this particular opponent for the entire tournament and noted that every time he'd had deuces through sixes in the first seat, he'd bring it in for $250, and then he'd show his hand on the end. So here he comes for $250, and I move in on him with two queens. This time he has two aces! It just goes to show you that any player, no matter how weak, can pick up a hand.

In Omaha high-low tournaments, if you're playing four-handed or less, which generally only happens at the final table, then you can play the big pairs. I won the Omaha high-low title at the World Series a few years ago with two nines over Chris Bjorin's two sixes, but unless you are playing very shorthanded, you shouldn't consider playing big pairs.

In a full ring game with so many of the cards out of the deck, those high-pair hands are nothing, but in a four-handed game there are only sixteen cards off the deck, leaving thirty-six still in it. Some of the cards your opponents need may never come out, and there are also a lot more cards left that can't hurt you. So even in Omaha high-low you can play those big pairs in four-handed tournament situations. But in a full ring game where the opposite is true—thirty-six cards out with only sixteen left in the deck—almost any card that comes off the deck is going to help somebody.

Trap Hands

Trap hands are hard to get away from. They look like winners, but usually turn out to be losers. Seldom if ever play trap hands in Omaha high-low.

Trap Hand #1

Hands such as 3-4-5-6 are trap hands. Here's why: If you get any action on the hand in a three- or four-way pot and the flop comes 7-2-K, you might think that you have a pretty good low draw. But if somebody plays with you, he probably has an

A-3 in his hand, and you're in real bad shape. You want to stay away from these types of rundown hands: 7-6-5-4, 8-7-6-5, 6-5-4-3.

THREE RANDOM TRAP HANDS TO AVOID

7-6-5-4
8-7-6-5
6-5-4-3

Even 5-4-3-2 can be a trap, because it looks just good enough to play if you're willing to draw to the 2-3 for low. A lot of people are going to play 2-3-4-5 because they're hoping to catch an ace on the flop and because they know they shouldn't play an aceless 2-3 hand unless they also have the 4-5. However, if no ace comes on the flop, you're left with only the third best low to draw to.

And then what do you do with the hand?

Of course, like everything else in life, there are exceptions to the rule. For example, in one Omaha high-low tournament I was in the big blind, and the game was at the $150/$300 level. I had been watching the players all day long, so I knew the hands they had been playing. A player raised from early position and there were three callers to me. I had J-10-9-7, a hand that I would just throw in the muck 99 times out of 100. But I thought, "None of these guys are playing these kinds of cards. They have all the low cards and all the super-high cards, so those sixteen cards are gone already. I'm gonna take a flop to this hand for $300. If it comes with middle cards, I'm the one who has them."

The flop came 8-9-4, the turn was a queen, and they all called the action.

"Let's put a king out there now," I said to myself, calling for my ideal card. Sure enough, there it came, and I wound up scooping the pot.

T.J.

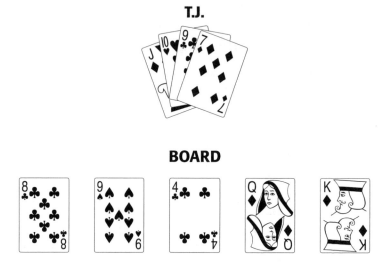

BOARD

Now, why did I play this hand? First, I knew how the other guys played, the kinds of cards they came in with. Second, I couldn't be raised, so I decided to take a shot with the hand. This isn't something that I recommend doing, but if you want to get a hold of some chips in a tournament, you take some chances once in a while.

Although I might have made the same play in a cash game, remember that when people can go to their pockets, they play a lot of strange hands, so it might not be too smart to play those kinds of cards. But in a tournament it's different. In tournaments, the kinds of cards people play is pretty cut and dried.

This is why you have to be a little more flexible at times in tournaments. You have an advantage when you have a pretty fair idea what cards they have, and they do not have an idea about what you have. Then when you have cards that you're fairly certain are live and it won't cost you much, you might play a hand that you wouldn't otherwise play.

It all depends on how the game is being played at your table at that time. Every player is different. Every table is different. In the postmortems of every tournament, you hear players say, "He shouldn't have played that hand," or "How could he have raised with those cards?"

People have different styles of play, but there is a "right" style, too, and that is what we're getting at in this book.

Trap Hand #2

K-Q-J-6: three high cards with a dangler. Who the hell wants to play that kind of hand? I've seen players with hands like that in the small blind call half a bet in an unraised pot, but why waste the money? The only time you should play this type of hand is when you're in the big blind and it's in an unraised pot.

Suppose you're in the small blind for $200 in a tournament. The limits are at the $400/$800 level. You've got three high cards and a dangler, but since it only costs you $200 to complete the bet, you do so. But if you don't flop anything to your K-Q-J-6 or Q-J-10-5, that's $200 lost. Had you saved that bet, a few hands later you might have found yourself in a later position, getting four-way action (including yourself). Now that $200 would have become $800. You could have eventually won $600 or $800 with that $200 you lost. You have to think about these things all the time, because in tournament play you can't go to your pocket.

Always Think Like a Pilot and Fly Ahead of the Plane

In other words, always think in advance about the consequences of your play. "If I make this call and lose $300 of my $1,000 in chips, I'll have $700 left. If I double up my $1,000 I'll have $2,000, but if I doubled up $700 I'd only have $1,400." The idea is to get all the chips, so you need to take all of these factors into consideration every time you make a decision. Actually, you shouldn't even have to think about it—once you know these concepts, many of your decisions should come automatically.

You shouldn't have to spend a lot of time when deciding whether to call, also known as making a **long call**. It should come automatically, quickly. You should be on automatic pilot, so to speak. Hopefully, after reading this book, you'll be able to develop your own automatic pilot mode.

PLAYING ON THE FLOP

If you flop the nuts and you can't be counterfeited, you can let your opponents come to you. If you don't have the stone nuts, you'll have to gamble a little bit. If the flop comes with two low cards and you have four low cards working toward the nuts, you'll be playing the hand and you'll be playing it strong.

Position really doesn't matter in a situation like that. The only thing that position does is provide you with more information. If you're **there**—that is, if you've made your hand—you might be able to start maximizing your bets. But of all the games I've played, I think that Omaha high-low is the least positional game there is. This is a hand-dominated game.

That's because so many people find an excuse to be in the pot that making a late-position raise, or even an early-position raise, doesn't have nearly the impact that it does in other games. Plus, Omaha high-low is a limit game.

The More People in the Pot, the Less Important Your Position is

> Omaha high-low is the least positional game there is. This is a hand-dominated game.

In almost any limit game, the importance of position depends on the number of players who are in the pot with you. The more players in the pot, the less important position becomes, and the more important hand value becomes. In limit hold'em, it is important to consider your position if you're playing heads-up. If your opponent checks to you in a heads-up hand, you might be able to represent something that will make him throw his hand away. But if there are three or four players still in the pot, chances are you won't be able to make all of them fold. Because it's a limit game and because most pots are played multiway, Omaha high-low is a hand-value game. On the other hand, in pot-limit Omaha, even with three or four players in the pot, position is so much more important than it ever will be in any limit game.

Therefore, I suggest that you play your hand straightforward in Omaha high-low most of the time. A lot of people trap in this game when they have huge hands, but those big hands don't come out very often. In most situations, simply bet your hand because position is never as important as it is in a pot-limit or no-limit game.

Reading the Board

You have to be a good reader in Omaha high-low. There are so many times when you can tell by the action that you might get only a fourth of the pot or less with your ace-deuce, so it's not worth putting your money in. You know that you have a nut low, but you also know that there are a couple of other nut lows out there after the flop.

Suppose the flop comes with two spades, and you can't make a flush. But say you have a good shot at the nut low—or you already have the nut low—and the action that tells you that one of your opponents has a set, another has the spade draw, and a couple of others have an ace-deuce, along with you. A lot of times, you might as well just throw that hand away, especially if you don't have another low card to go with your ace-deuce.

Why get involved with it if the best you probably can do is get a third of the low end?

When You Flop the Nut Straight

Suppose you're in the big blind in an unraised pot and you have middle cards. The flop comes out and you make the nut straight. How do you play it?

If no pair and three different suits are on board, you might want to push the hand very strongly. But if there are three flush cards out there, you'd better forget it. If the flop comes with two of a suit, you would play your straight a little slower until fourth street at least, because if the third suited card comes, it will probably make a flush for somebody. Remember that you can flop the nuts and lose it on the turn.

What if you flop a straight draw? If the flop comes out with a pair and two to your middle straight draw, you'd better play it very softly, if at all.

"If it's possible, it's probable" is the expression that Dana Smith used in her book for low-limit Omaha high-low players. The whole idea is that if you're playing against one person, the probability of your hand holding up is a lot higher than it is if you're in a multiway pot. So, you have to keep in mind the number of players in the pot.

Remember that with four cards working in the hands, there will always be more flushes, sets, and full houses out there. The nuts will almost always be there, especially in eight-or-better games. That's particularly true in low-limit games where so many pots are played multiway. And as we said earlier, when you play four high or semi-high straight cards, you always want to have two cards that can make a straight to the ace, so you at least need to have a J-10 in the hand.

Middle-Straight Hands

Example 1

Now let's look at another middle-straight hand. Suppose you are in the big blind in an unraised, multiway pot and you have this hand:

YOU

The flop comes:

FLOP

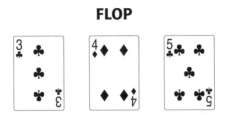

You've flopped the nuts. You know the ace-deuce hands are probably out and the players holding them have made a wheel. How do you play the hand? With two of a suit out there, just check and call.

Example 2

Now, what if you have this hand in the same situation:

YOU

The flop comes:

FLOP

Again, you have the nut straight, this time with an all-high board. What do you do? Same thing—check and call. As in Example 1, your hand is only the nuts at the moment.

In Example 1, who's going to make a higher straight than you? Nobody. In Example 2, it's the same concept: Nobody can make a higher straight than yours. But when two of the same suit are on the board and there's any action on the flop, there's a chance that the flush draw is out—or possibly a set— so why not play this hand slow to start with? If the third suited card doesn't show up on fourth street and there's only one card to come, then play it strong. You just have to use your head in these situations.

Example 3: A Tournament Hand

This time, let's look at a hand that was played in a five-way, unraised pot in a $100 buy-in Omaha high-low tournament. The lady in the big blind held:

YOU

The flop came:

FLOP

She checked the nut low from up front, and it was bet and called all the way around. She also flat called. The turn came with the 6♣. Again she checked and it was bet and called all the way around and again she also called. On the river came the J♣. This time she bet first, and only one player called. She scooped the pot with the nut low and a pair of eights.

BOARD

By betting first on the river, she represented the backdoor flush, and of course, she had a lock on the nut low. Later, she asked my opinion on how she had played the hand.

I analyzed it this way: Why didn't she lead at this pot on the flop, especially since she had a pair to go with the nut low? But since she decided to check on the flop, why didn't she raise after it was bet and the action came back to her? In limit poker, it is almost 90 percent "pure" that anyone who calls a bet on the flop will call a raise on the flop. It happens all the time. If you check with this hand, you do it for only one reason: to check-raise it and maximize the money in the pot. And from that point on, you have to bet first. If her nut low had been counterfeited on fourth street, she could've simply thrown it away.

If she hadn't had a pair to go with the nut low, it would have been correct for her to check and call, but the 8 gave her an extra out. And even if another 8 comes on fourth street, there'd be a pretty good chance that nobody filled up since there was no significant action on the flop. But having checked on the flop, she definitely should have bet out on the turn, especially when a random card, a jack, came.

By leading with the nut low on fourth street after checking it on the flop, you create confusion in your opponents' minds. They don't know what that turn card has done for you, if anything. Plus, since the bets are doubled on fourth street, some people who might have called the single bet on the flop might not call the bet on fourth street. If those opponents fold, it reduces the field of people drawing against you.

You also played the hand in a rather unorthodox way, adding to their confusion and making them guess. When you put your opponents to the guess, they usually guess wrong.

This is a good example of a situation where good players will always maximize their win. This player could have won at least four more bets on the hand if she'd have played it our way.

When the Flop Comes with Wheel Cards

Suppose the pot has been raised before the flop and you have called the raise with:

YOU

The action is now four-handed and the flop comes with:

FLOP

Someone in an early position bets, and you're next to act. Since your deuce was counterfeited on the flop, you now have a pair and an inside wheel draw. Do you call?

Of course not! Anytime you're certain that someone has already made a wheel, why would you call? You're only going for a split, meaning that even if you catch a 3, you'll only win half the pot at the best. Plus one of your opponents will probably make a higher straight, so you'll wind up with a fourth of the pot.

Players in low-limit games make these types of calls all the time. Of course, you want to see your opponents make this play, especially if you're the person with the wheel.

Suppose you have the same hand as in the first example and the flop comes with three wheel cards, two of them in your suit:

FLOP

You haven't made a wheel, but you have the nut flush draw. Do you draw? If you're certain that somebody has already made the wheel, you're throwing the hand away. In Omaha high-low the idea is to scoop pots. Anytime you can scoop a pot, you're ahead of the game. So, if you have to call a raise cold with nothing but a draw and you think there's already a wheel out there, there's hardly any reason to play further. Even if you make a set on the flop, you'll probably use the same strategy.

In this same four-way pot, suppose someone leads at the flop, the next player just flat calls, and now it's up to you.

Do you call?

Theoretically, no. If the player who flat-called cannot be counterfeited, he probably wouldn't raise on the flop; he'd wait to raise on fourth street, where the bets are double.

In this scenario, you might call the single bet. You have the nut-flush draw, and it's only going to cost you one single bet with at least two and possibly three other people in the pot. Of course, you're taking the risk that the player behind you might raise.

Now here's where position can become important in Omaha high-low: If you're the last to act, you can call the bet because you're thinking, "Since the action is in front of me, if the wheel is out, I'll know it on fourth street."

If someone has the wheel, he will certainly raise it on fourth street when the bets double. But if you're in early position, you won't have the advantage of watching what the other players do before deciding on your own play. The final word is this: If it isn't raised, there's nothing wrong with making a call, but if you believe the wheel is out, just throw the hand away.

When in Doubt, Dump it

Always go with your instincts. Use what you've learned over the years. Here's a good rule of thumb for Omaha high-low: Any time you're in doubt about a hand, dump it.

A lot of players will catch such a monster flop that they don't want to lose anybody. Maybe it comes with two of a suit and two wheel cards, and they have the complete wrap wheel draw with the nut-flush draw. Naturally, they don't want to lose anybody early. Even if they make it on fourth street, they won't raise; they'll wait until fifth street because they want to get at least one bet out of you on the end. And

> Any time you're in doubt about a hand, dump it

when the limits go up in a tournament, that isn't a bad play at all because they can win a lot of money on the end.

Playing a High Hand

If you have the high hand and you know that you're up against one or more low hands, you're going to be very, very aggressive with it. Any time you have the high—except when you flop a straight with two suited cards on board, as we discussed earlier—you should be rammin' and jammin,' just hoping a couple of players are drawing for low.

But suppose you've had the high hand all along with a couple of opponents drawing at the low. On the river comes a third low card and somebody fires a bet in front of you. You know that you have half of the pot in your pocket, but there's a player left to act behind you. In this scenario, a flat call might be better than a raise because you want to entice the third player to overcall, especially if you think he also has a low.

However, if you're the last to act when there's been a bet and a call in front of you, you definitely should raise in order to maximize your win. You don't care if there's a reraise and the third guy folds, because you're still going to win the same amount of money.

Let me put it this way: If you're in last position in a tournament, your mother is sitting to your left, and she's the one who led at the pot and got two callers, you raise! "Mom, you've just gotta learn how to play better!" is what Tom would say.

Playing a Drawing Hand in a Side Game

When you have a strong draw in Omaha high-low, and you're in a front position, how far do you take it? I'd bet it on the flop but I'm not saying that I would bet it on fourth street where it's a double bet. I like to lead on the flop with it—that's fine. And if you're playing heads-up, there's nothing wrong with leading at it again on fourth street. But if I'm in a multiway pot, I shut down on fourth.

You see, when you're against only one other guy, betting on fourth street sets up a bet on fifth street if you think he's going low. But against two or three other players, betting on fourth street doesn't set anything up for you. One of your opponents might be playing high and the other one might be playing low, so you're in a different situation. I'm not saying that you don't call, just that you don't lead at the pot. Actually, you're hoping to get a free card.

But you see so many people continue to push their draws in the lower-limit games, $4/$8 up to $10/$20. If you want to play Omaha high-low the right way, here are some basic concepts:

Never be overly aggressive unless you have a very strong hand on the flop

Make all your moves later in the play—always at the double-bet level

Remember that when you raise at one of the two-bet levels, it's worth a lot more to you

If a guy has a lot of money invested in the pot he'll usually call that extra bet.

Delaying Your Action

Only sophisticated players with a lot of discipline will delay their action until fourth or fifth street. Players with average skills who just like betting the nuts all the time don't realize that they sometimes can make more money by delaying their action. But that's part of adjusting to the game, too.

If you're in a game where everybody's calling everything all the way through, why not lead with your hand? You don't have to wait until fourth or fifth streets because you're going to get them to play anyway. But when you're in there against some decent players, a lot of times you'll delay your action so you can get as much as possible out of the pot. The caliber of your opposition always affects your strategy.

Saving Bets

In the limit hold'em games, you'll see an opponent with an ace lead at the pot when it gets checked to him. If he gets raised, he automatically calls. Ninety-nine out of a hundred players will call that first raise. He might only have an ace against your set, but he's going to try to catch an ace for himself when there's a low flop. Sometimes it works for him, but I'll bet that if he charted his play over a year's time, he'd find that he's a losing player.

Remember that in all limit games, unless you've had a rush of cards, the bets you save will be what you win at the end of the day. While X, Y, and Z have been making those long calls, you haven't—and that's going to be your profit margin at the end of the day. The cards will break even over a long period of time.

Say that you have the nut flush draw and the nut low draw on the flop. Am I saying that you should check if you're in early position and you don't make it on the turn? You're damn right I am—in limit games.

In no-limit games, one of the worst plays you can make is to be in last position and bet a draw with one card to come, when you could've seen it for nothing. You've wasted a bet. The same concept is true in Omaha high-low. On fourth street with one card to come, take your free draw if you're around back and nobody has bet. Why waste the bet?

If you have a strong drawing hand on the flop and it's checked to you, I'd certainly go ahead and bet it. A lot of times, you'll get the free card anyway because you have bet on the flop. But if you had checked on the flop, your opponents may feel more free to bet into you on the turn, forcing you to call the double bet to see the river card. So it's actually cheaper for you to make the one-unit bet on the flop.

Getting a Free Card

Here's a situation where position comes into play. Say that you're around back and have a drawing hand on the flop. If someone bets into you, you raise it. Almost invariably, that raise will give you the free card on fourth street. If your opponent called your bet on the flop, he'll think that you're the one with the strong hand going and check to you on fourth street. If you don't make your hand on fourth, you check along.

This is a limit hold'em play, but it works in any limit game when you want to get a free card. Note that I say "free card," but this is actually a "half-a-bet card" because you've raised on the flop.

Here's the beauty of it: Your opponents will be unsure whether or not you were on a draw, so if you make the hand, they very well may call you on the end. Some players will check it to get the call on the end, even if they make the hand on fourth street.

That's an ultra-sophisticated play and it works well against either very bad players or very good players, because it creates confusion. At the same time, we could name more than 100 players who play it the same way every time. You *know* that if your opponent checked on fourth street when the flush card came and then bet on fifth street, he made the flush and checked it on fourth. You can get away from opponents like that because you know they play exactly the same way every time. That's why you have to change your play around a little bit.

Playing a Drawing Hand in a Tournament

Consider the situation that Dana Smith found herself in when playing in a $200 buy-in Omaha high-low tournament.

She had an A-2-5-7 in a heads-up pot, and a 3-4-10 flopped with no suits. Her opponent checked and she bet.

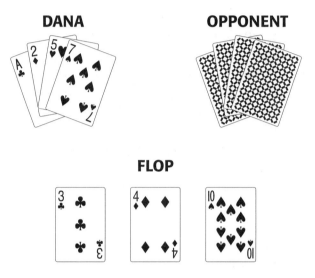

DANA   **OPPONENT**

FLOP

On the turn she didn't make her draw, the opponent checked, and she bet it again, thinking that since he was a strong player he wouldn't call if he didn't have a hand. But he called. On the river the board paired and Dana had nothing. When he bet first, she released the hand.

Did she make the right play?

Yes, she had no choice but to fold. But what would you do if her opponent had checked at the river? What if, just like her, he had just been drawing for the low? In a multiway pot, you wouldn't bet it on the end, and you wouldn't have bet on fourth street either.

But heads-up, why not? This is where the iron balls come in!

Strong Players versus Weak Players

Remember that a weak player usually won't call you if he doesn't have anything. There's a better chance that a strong player will call you on the end than there is that a weak player will. If the weak player knows he has nothing, he'll say, "Well, I can't beat anything." But the strong player might have an A-K, no pair—or anything, for that matter—and call you. All top players have made this play.

I'll give you an example from a hold'em game with a lesson that applies not only to Omaha, but to all poker games. In a one-table hold'em satellite, the board came 2♦ 2♥ 3♣. I was in the big blind with J♦ 6♠. The player right in front of me bet his hand and I called him. The turn came nothing. He bet, and I called again. On the end, he bet again and I called him and took the pot with a jack high.

Then a player says, "I want to learn how to make that play!"

Jim Ward recognized the play and leaned over to me and said, "The funny thing is, they think it's luck when you do that."

Although I knew the other player and thought he was out of line, I never raised at any time. I believed my jack high was best and I wanted him to keep coming. I had put a dead read on the guy. All he could have had to bet with was a 4-5 for a straight draw or something like that. It's just another situation that shows how important it is to know your opponents.

PLAYING ON THE TURN

Suppose you are in a front position in a multiway pot and you have:

YOU

The flop comes 3-5-K. You bet and two people call. The turn comes with a deuce, so the board reads:

BOARD

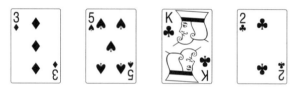

Your low draw is counterfeited and there are three wheel cards on the board. What do you do?

If I were against only one opponent who I think is semi-weak, I might consider betting to see his reaction. But if there are players left to act behind me in a multiway pot and there are three wheel cards on the board, I would check.

You should mainly be concerned with not standing a raise with this hand, so you check the turn. If someone bets behind you, you fold the hand. After all, what do you have? It's not smart to play bottom two pair and an inside wheel draw against an opponent who may already have the wheel and possibly another player who thinks he can draw out with the top two pair.

Bluffing

Here's a question a lot of people ask: "When your low draw gets counterfeited, couldn't you just go ahead and bet again on fourth street to represent the wheel—especially since you had bet first on the flop?"

Let me tell you something about bluffing in limit Omaha high-low—it's ridiculous! I don't mean that you can never do it. There are certain situations where you can run a bluff, but the situation described above isn't one of them.

Now suppose you know that your opponent has a low draw because of the way he has played the hand. A set comes on the board at the end, and there is no low possibility, which means the best hand is the fourth card of that rank or the highest pair held in any player's hand. If you're up against only one opponent and he's been leading in the hand, you might bluff at this pot. Since you pretty well know that he doesn't have any pairs, you might just win this hand with a bet on the end. This is one bluff you can make in Omaha high-low, but there are very few others.

Here's another example of a bluff, this one in a $20/$40 game. Tom was in an unraised pot in late position with a rundown hand that he normally wouldn't play, 5-6-7-9 suited. The flop came 8-4-Q. It was bet and called in two places, and Tom called with the inside straight draw. The turn card paired the 4. The original bettor checked, as did everybody else, including Tom. On the river came a jack, making the board 8-4-Q-4-J with the possibility of a straight.

TOM

BOARD

Everybody had missed the low. When they all checked to Tom, he bet. One by one, they folded. This type of positional play sometimes works when you're certain that no one has made a hand either way. There is only one downside to this play. What if someone had flopped two pair, made the full house on the turn, and checked twice with the intent of check-raising anybody who bet?

Tom's opponents were playing quite straightforwardly so he didn't think that was the case, although the double check is a play that a sophisticated player might make in this situation. In addition, a certain breed of very sophisticated player might have figured out that he was trying to steal the pot and check-raised with nothing!

However, Tom had read his opponents correctly and no one figured out his play.

Less Than the Nuts

Are there times when you should call with less than the nuts? For example, should you call with an A-3 when the board comes with three low cards? If you have an A-10-3-4 (or 5) with the ace suited, how could you not play your low draw? The A-2 isn't always out, you know.

This is a case where the preflop action would determine the strategy. Say nobody had raised and Tom flopped the second-nut low with my A-3. If it is checked to him and he's in late position, he would bet it. If there had been any preflop raises and he's in an early position, he probably would check it. If everyone checked on the flop, he would lead with it on fourth street and bet it at the river most of the time.

The Theory and the Reality

Since there is so much difference between the way that low-limit and high-limit Omaha high-low games are played, does that mean that in the low-limit games, you usually need to have the nuts to be in the pot whereas, in the higher limit games you don't?

Yes. In the higher-limit games there usually are fewer people involved in the pot than there are in lower-limit games, strictly because of the amount of money involved. Remember, the more people in the pot, the more likely it is that somebody has the nuts. In low-limit games, players are peddling the nuts a lot more often than they are in higher-limit games.

In theory, the play of your hands should not be determined by the size of the limits, but in reality, you have to adjust to the size of the game and how your opponents are playing it. If you have a shot at the nuts in a lower-limit game, you might take a few more chances with your starting hands and on the flop because it won't cost you much. But, in a higher-limit game it can cost you a bundle. Furthermore, you'll be up against a lot of maniacs in low-limit games, which changes the flow of everything.

Therefore, in lower limit games, you can play looser before the flop, but you should play tighter after the flop, whereas in higher-limit games you play tighter before the flop and a little looser after the flop.

Again, in theory you should play the same no matter what the limits, but in actuality I don't know anybody who doesn't play a little looser in the smaller games. If a great high-limit player sits down in a little low-limit game, his game might go to pot. Like Stuey Ungar used to say, "I've got no chance playing $5/$10 limit hold'em. No chance whatsoever."

Fancy Moves

Are any fancy moves possible at the lower limit games? Sometimes, but not very often. Let me tell you about a pretty good move that came down in a game. I missed my low and ended up with two pair, top and third, on the end. I knew that somebody had made a low. The man on my right bet. I called because I thought I had the high hand, and then the obvious low hand raised the pot, opening it up. The man on my right, who had both the nut low and the same two pair that I held, reraised to knock me out of the pot. He accomplished his mission. I give the guy an A+ for the play. He didn't have the nut high, but he figured that the reraise would knock me out if I also didn't have the nuts. So, instead of winning half of the pot (one quarter for low and one quarter for high), he won three-fourths of it.

In the low-limit games, there are more players per pot but they're more passive. They limp in more often, whereas in the higher-limit games there is more raising, more aggression. They thin out the pot more often before the flop with their raises. In the lower-limit games, the raise is used for two reasons: to build the pot and to limit the field, but in the higher-limit games the raise is mostly used to thin the field.

Getting Trapped with the Second-Nut Low

In Omaha high-low, a lot of people fall into the trap of hanging on with the second-nut low against heavy action on the flop or turn. Suppose a 3-4-5 is on the board, and someone has an A-6 in his hand.

PLAYER

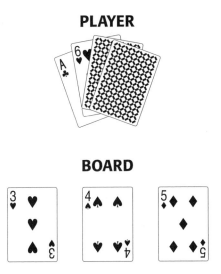

BOARD

Some players just won't cut themselves loose from the hand. There may be all sorts of action on fourth street, but they play the hand anyway, even though they have no outs. The wheel is out there and if the board is suited, somebody else probably has a flush.

Why? Sometimes it happens after the opponent bets and the player with A-6 calls. Then the action takes place behind the player and he'll say, "Well, I called the first bet so I might as well call the next one."

Then he's hooked into the pot.

Just remember that if you're in a multiway pot with an A-6 in this situation, you'd better dump the hand. Shane Smith's advice is well stated: "If it's possible, it's probable."

PLAYING ON THE RIVER

You could have the biggest draw in the world—the best high wraparound or the nut flush draw along with a wheel draw—and still wind up with nothing in Omaha high-low. Sometimes it seems that Omaha high-low this is the biggest draw-out game in the world. That's one of the things that lures so many people into playing Omaha high-low. And that's also why it's so important to have an extra out, a second hand that you can draw to.

Always Try to Have an Extra Out

What happens when you've had the nut low all along and get counterfeited on the river, meaning you're left with only the second-nut low? How you play it depends on the action.

If you're first to bet, you'll have to check and then decide upon your best move based on the action after you. But suppose you've been counterfeited for the nut low and all hell breaks loose in front of you—for example, there's a bet and a raise before it gets to you, or there is a bet and a couple of callers. With substantial action in front of you, you have to reevaluate whether your hand is worth a play. If there's a bet and a raise, especially if the raise comes from someone that you suspect is on a low hand, your hand should automatically become history.

However, say that a player who you think is on a high hand leads at the pot and only one or two others call but they don't raise. In this case, your hand may be worth an overcall, mainly because one of the callers may have a weaker low, or at the least, a hand that ties yours. Therefore, it's worth a bet even if you get only a quarter of the pot since the pot is substantial in size.

What you can't do is to call a bet and a raise, or put yourself in danger of being raised after you have acted. For example, suppose someone leads into the pot at the river and you are next to act with two or three people yet to act behind you. You have to pass because you're in danger of getting raised and/or reraised. You can't take the chance of throwing in a bet because you can't handle a raise—unless you have a dead read that no one is likely to raise you. All you can do in this situation is make a crying call for one single bet and even then, if a rock still to act looks like he's going to make a long call, you'd better reevaluate. Sometimes the rocks won't put in a raise with the nut low or second-nut low because they're afraid of getting quartered, so you have to use judgment.

As a general rule, when I have the second-nut low at the river and the pot is substantial, you should call if it only costs you one more bet and you think there's a reasonable chance that you'll get at least a quarter of the pot.

Determining the Best High Hand

If somebody bets and two or three players just call in front of you at the river, it can be difficult to determine whether the callers have a low hand or a high hand. Let's assume that the first bettor has a high hand. If no flushes or straights are possible, it may be difficult for a high hand to know for sure whether he has the best high, so he might call with a hand that he thinks might take the high half of the pot. If you have a low hand but have been counterfeited, you may still have the best low or be tied for it, even when someone bets and two players call in front of you.

In fact, the best high is more difficult to determine than the best low. You always know where you are on the low, because you know what the best possible low hand is. But you don't always know whether your high hand is the best. Suppose the board reads A-6-J-4-9. The best low is 2-3, and the best possible high is trip aces. But the best high hand being played by an opponent could be trip jacks, or top two pair, or even bottom set.

It's easy to read the nut low but it isn't always clear what the high is. Sometimes the best high is an overpair, a weak two pair, a low set, or maybe even a one-pair hand. Other times, a high hand might lead at the pot and an even better high hand will only smooth call because he wants all of the lows in there so he can get a half of their money. And the nut lows often use that same strategy to win a bigger half of the pot.

Betting the Nut Low

You cannot bet the low on the end if that's all you have. You don't have to "know" that there's another low hand out there, or even that there's a probability of its being out there—you can sense it.

However, you can bet it if you're playing against one other person that you think might be drawing for high and you think that you might be able to scoop the pot from him. For example, maybe you have a pair along with the low or maybe you don't even have a pair, but you think you can get by with representing one.

Some low-limit players insist on betting the nut low with nothing else, even if it's obvious to any decent player that there's another nut low out. This happens in tournaments all the time. Good players will simply check. For example, a player told me about an Omaha high-low tournament he once played. In one hand, he flopped the nut low up front in a multiway pot and check-called the hand all the way. On the river the button raised, he called, and so did a third player. The button turned over the nut low and the two of them were quartered by the high hand. "Man, how could you have kept checking that nut low?" the button asked him.

He told me that he usually lets everything go by but that every now and then he'll get his dander up and put people in their place. In this case, he gave his opponent the standard answer: "Buddy, when you learn how to play this game, come back and ask me that question again."

The main point is this: If you've been betting the low hand in a pot where there's been three-way action all the way—and you know there's one high hand—you cannot bet your low hand on the end because you're probably getting quartered. When you only have a one-way hand, you're making more money for the other guy than you are for yourself!

A Move on the River in a Tournament

In a $300 buy-in Omaha high-low tournament Dana Smith was holding the 2♣ 6♦ 7♣ 10♦ in the big blind in an unraised pot, and there were two other players in the hand. At this point there were only three tables left and the limits were quite high. She didn't know the player in the middle but she knew the guy in third position to be an aggressive, high-limit cash game player. The flop came with A♠ Q♦ 5♣. Dana checked, the middle man bet, and the third player and Dana both called.

On the turn came the 9♣, giving her an inside-straight draw, a low draw, and a weak four-flush. Again, it was check, bet, call, call. The river card was the Q♣.

DANA   **OPPONENT**

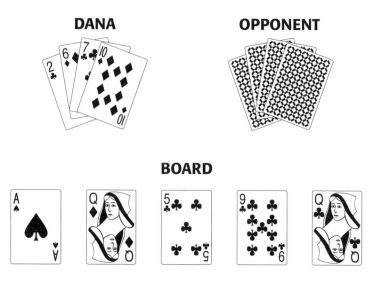

BOARD

Dana checked, the second player bet, and the third player raised. She thought about calling, but with no low and only a little flush against what was probably a full house, she decided to fold. The player in the middle called with an A-10. The third played showed an A-K. Neither had a flush or full-house— not even a set! The third man simply made a move at the pot, that's all.

Even though she lost the pot, Dana's play was right, and it is a good example of an important concept: If you cannot lay down a winner in poker, you're a calling station and you cannot win. Remember that.

> If you cannot lay down a winner in poker, you're a calling station and you cannot win.

POT-LIMIT
OMAHA

POT-LIMIT OMAHA

T.J. Cloutier

Pot-limit Omaha is the biggest money game played today. A game of pot-limit Omaha is about three or four times the size of a game of pot-limit hold'em with the same size blinds, and when it is played, it usually is the biggest poker game in the casino. A few Southern California cardrooms are now spreading it. The blinds in their pot-limit hold'em games are $10/$20, and the blinds in the pot-limit Omaha games are $5/$10, but if the casinos really wanted the two games to be about the same size, they'd make the blinds $15/$30 or even $20/$40 in the hold'em games and $5/$10 in the Omaha games.

Although it is the most treacherous poker game of all, pot-limit Omaha is also the best game for making a big score. If you can get lucky, catch some cards and flops, and play right, you can make more money in this game than you can in any other.

Players who love pot-limit Omaha will travel long distances for a tournament even though they have very little interest in playing the actual events. They are interested in the fact that all the big pot-limit players will be at the tournament and that they'll probably be able to get a few side games going.

At the World Series a few years ago, we played a pot-limit Omaha game with $100/$200 blinds with an $8,000 buy-in, and a $200/$400 game with a $20,000 buy-in. And the games were full all the time! I played and so did Sammy Farquhar, Lindy Chambers, Howard Greenspan, Roger Moore, Tony

Dee, Eskimo Clark, Phil Hellmuth, and more. Of course, when we play that high, it's going to bust a lot of people. I played four nights in a row—never for more than two hours at a time—and I won $57,000. I suppose I could've won $157,000 in that length of time, but I could have lost that much, too, right?

Actually, I wouldn't have lost that much. Unlike a lot of the high-stakes players these days, I won't take chances and lose more money than I stand to win. As far as I'm concerned, that's the biggest fault in a lot of players. When they win a little bit, they quit. When they lose, they go for almost their whole bankroll. It's called eating like a bird and crapping like an elephant, which is easy to do in pot-limit Omaha.

Now let's move forward and discuss nine of the most important concepts in pot-limit Omaha.

NINE MOST IMPORTANT POT-LIMIT OMAHA CONCEPTS

1. Have the Best Hand with a Draw to a Better Hand

Pot-limit Omaha is the only game ever devised in which you can flop the nuts and have to throw it away on the flop! Suppose you flop the nut straight and you get action on it. If two suited cards are out there and you get more than one-way action on the hand, it means that someone probably has a set and someone else most likely has the nut-flush draw—you're a dog in this hand.

That's the difference between pot-limit and limit Omaha. In limit Omaha, where it costs only a one-unit bet, you play the hand and hope that nobody draws out on you. But in pot-limit Omaha you'll have to put in all that money and then pray that the hand holds up, so quite often the best thing to do is to dump it. All top tournament players have done that a zillion times.

How about a draw to the nut flush in pot-limit Omaha with no backup? For a lot of money, I think it would be a bad call, especially heads-up. Don't get me wrong: If you're getting big odds on your money it may be different. Sometimes there's a lot of money in the pot before the flop, and you're getting three- or four-way action. In that case if you flop the nut flush draw and all of the action is in front of you, you might want to continue. But you don't want to be the first man to act with this hand—you have to check it from up front because all you have is a draw.

Now let's say you flop the nut flush draw in a ring game and there's action in front of you. In this situation, you almost have to call the bet as long as you're in a big pot and you're willing to go to your pocket again. But in a tournament—unless you're short-stacked and just trying to get a hold of some chips—you simply couldn't call a bet, because if you lose, you're out of the tournament.

You can play a lot more hands after the flop in limit Omaha than in pot-limit. That's the difference between the two. You might take a draw in a limit game that you would not take in either a pot-limit game or a tournament. But in both games, it's always nice to have a backup draw.

2. Understand the Betting Structure

In many pot-limit cash games, the opening bet must be twice the big blind. For example, if the big blind is $100 in a side game, you have to bring it in for $200, and this is not a raise, just the opening bet. This rule prevents the blinds from getting a freeroll by forcing them to put more money in the pot to see the flop.

This isn't the case in tournaments, where you can come in for the same price as the big blind or **gypsy in**. However, most cardrooms want their side games to emulate the tournament structure, so they allow players to gypsy in when playing side games.

Some years ago, one of the biggest pot-limit Omaha games in the nation used to be played on the weekends at the Horseshoe in Tunica, Mississippi. They played $25/$50 blinds, and most of the players straddled it with $100, which means you can bring it in for four times the big blind or $400. If one guy calls $400 and another guy calls $400, now the next guy can call $400 and raise $1,600. If all four of them call for $1,600 there's $6,400 in the pot and the next bet can be $6,400 on the flop. If there is some play on the flop and it gets called, then you have three times that amount, which is $19,200 in the pot on the flop. You can see how it can tear you apart money-wise because it escalates quickly. Of course, it's fun to play if you really want to gamble. You'll find people gambling with some very strange hands, which is one reason why you'll always see more multiway action in pot-limit Omaha games than in pot-limit hold'em games.

When players want to compete for big money these days, they have a choice of pot-limit Omaha or no-limit hold'em, both of which have enjoyed surges in popularity that have brought them back into the limelight. Pot-limit Omaha is the best game to make money, but it's also the toughest game.

3. Don't Lose Your Whole Bankroll in One Session

No matter what game you are playing, you shouldn't lose your entire bankroll in any one poker session. The idea is to have enough discipline to quit and play another day, give yourself a chance. Don't be one of those players who ignores this advice and blows his entire bankroll time and time again.

I know a player from Texas who is so good at pot-limit Omaha, he will play for six months at a time and win every session. But he's the type of player who, if he has $100,000 and gets on a losing streak in the game, he'll lose it all in that one game. Then he'll fly home, get refinanced, and come back again. To me, this just does not make sense. Some people think that because they've gotten loser and managed to get their money back a couple of times, they can do it every time.

Very seldom do you get a **live one**, a person who can't play at all, playing in these big games, but it does happen sometimes. I know a player who, when he first came on the scene a few years ago and played high, would reraise with any four suited cards. It didn't matter what size they were or if they were connected. If the pot had been raised and three or four players were in it, he would reraise it. Everybody knew he was going to do this. He was just asking to go broke—and his opponents accommodated him. Of course, he put a lot of pressure on the game and he won a lot of pots because he got some funny flops, but in the long run, he had to lose.

Again, you have to use some discipline when you're playing cards, and he didn't have any.

4. Know the Implied Odds

Implied odds are the future bets that you can expect to win if you get the right flop to your hand, and your opponents do not read you correctly and give you too much action. A lot of pot-limit Omaha hands have much higher implied odds than do limit Omaha hands.

Sometimes if you play cards that aren't great starting hands in exactly the right situations against the right people, you can win gigantic pots in pot-limit games. For instance, if you have a small pair and can get in cheap with it, or if it will only cost you a tiny little raise, you have enormous implied odds with a little hand that you're not going to play further unless you catch a favorable flop. In this sense, pot-limit Omaha is somewhat like no-limit hold'em.

For example, suppose you have 9-8-7-6 or 8-7-6-5 and you know that your opponent has big stuff. You can call a modest bet. You can play this type of hand before the flop for a small raise, too. Remember that the pots start out small in pot-limit and don't get bigger until a couple of rounds of betting are already in the pot.

To summarize, when there's either a single minimum bet or a modest raise, you can play four connecting cards that you know aren't the best hand at the moment. In fact, if your opponent is a pretty solid player and you're sure that he has a big pair, you should be pleased to know that you have cards that are totally unrelated to his hand. Since it won't cost you an arm and leg to see the flop, you can call the bet or modest raise. Your opponent won't know for sure where you're at, but you'll know where he's at. You have big implied odds in this hand.

5. Be Careful When You Flop a Set

Easy does it when you flop a set. A set has less value in pot-limit Omaha than in any other poker game. The thing to remember about pot-limit Omaha is that when five cards are out, straights and flushes are usually going to be possible on the board. You can flop a set, even top set, and be a big dog if you get played with.

I'll never forget one time when Mansour Matloubi and I were in a game together. I raised with aces, and the flop came A♥ Q♣ 4♥. Mansour had K♥ J♥ 10♦ 9♦. If I don't pair the board, I'm a big dog in this hand, even though I have the best hand at the moment. I bet, he raised, and we got all the money in on the flop.

MANSOUR   **T.J.**

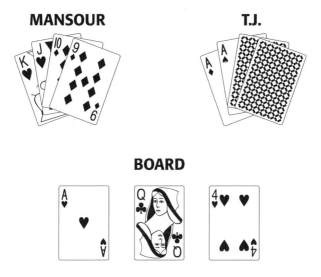

BOARD

"You can't win," Mansour says to me. "You have three aces and you can't win."

Well, I knew that I could win: He could rag off or the board could pair. But neither happened—the first card off made the straight for him and the river card made the flush.

Tom tells about a similar experience he had against Bob Ciaffone: "I flopped top set with pocket jacks and no straight or flush possible for me. Although two suited cards and a connecting card came on the flop, I had the nuts at that moment. He bet, I raised, and he put me in. 'Gee, I wish I had more money,' I mumbled. And Ciaffone says, 'Hey, Tom, if you like your hand that much, I'll let you go into your pocket for another $500.' I thought about it for a moment and said okay. Of course I lost. He had a gigantic wraparound straight draw plus a flush draw, and he knew exactly what I had, so he cheerfully allowed me to put more money into the pot."

Unless you're playing just one man, you'd better play very, very carefully with bottom set, even on a broken board. Say the flop comes J-7-3 and you have a pair of threes in the hole. Somebody starts firing at you. What are you going to do with this hand? What are you going to give him, 10-9-8?

YOU

OPPONENT

BOARD

If you raise him to build a pot, he can put a monster reraise on you. Then what do you do? What I'm saying is that you can play the hand on the flop but you don't have to raise with it. If you raise and get reraised, your trip threes are probably a piece of cheese, so be very careful when you flop bottom set.

6. Be Cautious When Raising in Tournaments

You don't have to build the pot before the flop—it will get big enough. This game can chew up your money so fast, it'll make your head spin. You play, you win four or five little pots of $500 to $1,000 each, you have $4,000 in front of you—and that entire $4,000 could be in the pot before the flop in the next big hand!

The man that I consider to be the best high-stakes Omaha player alive is Lyle Berman. I think he has the best mind for the game. He once told me that in any pot-limit Omaha tournament, there is no hand worth putting in the first raise before the flop. He's not suggesting that you don't reraise with aces double-suited to knock the field down to one player if you can. Of course, you can do that. But you seldom put in the first raise with any hand. When you think about it, do you know how often players get broke in tournaments and side games with two aces? An enormous number of times.

You see, that first raise is never big enough to shut people out. They know where you're at most of the time. That's why I might make a raise in a ring game with a 10-10-9-8, for example, from around back. I want them to put me on aces. And then I want to flop middle cards and see what happens.

What Lyle said is so true: If anybody has a decent playing hand, he's going to call the first raise at least. You can't knock anybody out with the first raise anyhow, so let *them* do the raising.

If you want to do something in pot-limit Omaha, look for a situation like the following: Three players are in the pot, somebody raises and then gets called in two spots. By this time there's enough money in the pot that you can either shut out all of your opponents—or all except one of them with a pot-sized reraise. The pot has to be big enough in to allow you to put in enough money to shut out the other players.

For example, suppose you find yourself in a situation where someone raises and a couple of players call. You have two aces with a couple of connecting cards. Now you can reraise, but you don't put in the initial raise yourself. You see, when there's a raiser and a couple of callers, then it's worth it to reraise with your aces and connectors or suits because the pot is big enough that your raise can shut somebody out and narrow it down to you and one other person.

In tournament play there are always exceptions to this strategy. If I am short-stacked, I'll be more likely to raise the maximum before the flop with aces, even if I am the first one in. Also, if I have a large stack against players with short or medium stacks, I will put the heat on them with aces, especially if I think that they are in survival mode. These are two of the rare cases where I'd raise early with aces in tournament play.

With exceptions such as these, I believe that Lyle's theory is so right: There is no hand good enough for a good player to make the first raise in pot-limit Omaha.

7. Get to Know Your Opponents

When you're playing in a pot-limit Omaha game or tournament where you don't know the players, you have to identify which players will raise before the flop with which kinds of hands. A lot of players will raise with aces with connectors or aces double-suited, and there are others who will raise with connecting cards like A-K-Q-J all the way down to 6-5-4-3. You have to know who will raise with what before the flop.

Having a backdoor draw helps sometimes, too. For example, when I'm playing against a guy who I know has aces, and I have a pair, a couple of three-flushes, or a **middle buster** (an inside straight draw) with second pair, I might go after the guy. But I'd have to have a dead read on him. This is where knowledge of your opponents, which we harped on in our first book, comes into play.

Here's something else you should find out about your opponents: Who will lead with a draw and who won't? Some players never make any moves, they just play the percentages. They're looking to show down the best hand every time. They wait forever to get big hands and hope to get a flop to their hands when they play them.

In pot-limit Omaha cash games and tournaments, I've won a lot of money in pots where, having put both of my opponents on aces, it didn't cost me very much to call the raise. When I know their aces are gone, I might play a hand such as 4-5-6-7 because I stand to win a big pot if I make the hand. I don't necessarily need this type of hand to be suited because I'd have to give my opponents credit for having suits, although it's still better to be suited than unsuited. Hands made up of three rundown cards and a pair—5-6-7-7, 5-5-6-7, and 5-6-6-7 for example—will take the aces right off a lot of times.

But here's the deciding factor when it comes to playing this type of hand: You must know in advance that both opponents are playing aces. And you don't want to see a pair on the board. You never want to see a pair come on the board in that situation unless it makes a set for you, because your opponents could win the hand with aces up.

Your opponents will "show" you what they're playing. Suppose one guy raises and the next guy reraises. You know that the first guy will only raise with aces and you know that if the second guy reraises, then he has aces for sure—because in pot-limit Omaha nobody reraises unless he has aces, except for certain maniacs who will raise or reraise with any four cards that are double-suited. In a ring game especially, if you have a hand like the ones I've mentioned, it's worth calling because you have a chance to win some big money. Your opponents have already put in a lot of money and if they get a small flop, they're coming with it. You won't have to lead to them—they're going to bet it for you! And this is exactly what you're looking for.

In every pot-limit Omaha tournament in which I've done well, at some point I've had a rundown hand with a pair against two people with aces or one opponent with aces and the other one with kings. I played the hand, caught a small or medium flop, and took them off their hands.

8. Learn to Judge the Size of Your Bets

How do you judge the size of your bets in pot-limit Omaha?

It's almost pure that you always raise the size of the pot if you have a hand. The idea that you should build the pot in pot-limit hold'em does not apply to pot-limit Omaha because Omaha pots get built automatically. Generally speaking, no one comes in for a raise that is less than the size of the pot. You don't see $500 in the pot and bet $100 at it.

In other words, a good player doesn't make a small bet to try to pick up a big pot. But you do occasionally see a bad player try that. Their underbet is a tip-off that they have a big hand and want to get called. An inexperienced player, or a weak player who's afraid he won't get paid off on a hand, might bet $100. But if you keep your bets standard rather than betting in some sort of pattern, your opponents won't be able to judge where you're at based on the size of your bet."

In pot-limit you can say, "I bet the pot." Then the dealer counts it down for you.

9. Understand the Principles of Taking Insurance

Insurance is fairly common in pot-limit poker, depending on who the players are, whether they like to gamble, and so on. Usually, insurance comes up when two guys are heads-up with a lot of money in the pot and one of them is all-in, and it is laid either on the flop or on fourth street.

In an insurance deal, the better hand will take odds against the worse hand drawing out on him. Then you figure out the number of outs the worse hand has. The guy with the best hand makes the main decisions—he makes an offer, and if his opponent wants to go with the deal they do insurance. If not, they don't do it. The leader doesn't have to offer insurance at all if he prefers to gamble with the hand.

You never get the true price on insurance. Let's say you have the nut flush draw and your opponent has a set. You have 18 outs to make the flush, unless he has two lower flush cards, in which case, you're down to 7 x 2 or 14 outs. An even hand has 28 outs, so your opponent is a 2 to 1 favorite with two cards to come. And with one card to come, you have 7 outs versus 28, so he is a 4 to 1 favorite.

The player in the lead with the best hand is the one who asks for insurance. If you are in the lead and ask for insurance, you have to be willing to give up some of the price. For example, if you're a 2 to 1 favorite, you probably can get 8 to 5 at the best. If you're a 4 to 1 favorite, you might get 3 to 1 insurance, tops.

Here is another type of insurance: With $5,000 in the pot, the underdog says, "You take $3,000, I'll take $1,000 and we'll play for the other $1,000."

In addition a player who isn't in the hand might ask to lay you insurance, saying, "I'll lay you 8 to 5, what do you want it for? I'll lay you $8,000 to $5,000." If you win the pot, you have to give him $5,000. If you lose it, he gives you $8,000. If the insurance proposition is 2 to 1, you have to give him $5,000 if you win, but he has to give you $10,000 if you lose.

Another form of insurance that is very popular these days involves running the cards twice. You might do it on fourth and fifth streets or on fifth street only. Suppose all the money's in and now you want to do insurance. You have the draw and your opponent has the hand. Then somebody says, "Okay, we'll run 'em twice."

When you run them twice, you're playing for half the pot each time. The dealer burns and turns, burns and turns, and then you figure out who won the first deal. If the board rags off on the end, your opponent wins one-half of the pot. But if you make the flush the first time around, then he has another chance to beat you on the second deal. Then those cards are taken away and the dealer burns and turns, burns and turns again, and then you figure out who won on the second deal.

Obviously, if you do insurance on fifth street only, you burn and turn only one card, but you are still playing for a half of the pot. Sometimes, they will run the deal three times, by burning and turning three times in a row. In this case, you have a chance to win one-third of the pot each time.

I remember one time when I was playing pot-limit hold'em against Betty Carey. On fourth street the board shows K-J-8-5. I have kings and jacks and she has kings and fives with one card to come. The odds are 21 to 1 in my favor. Betty says, "I'll give you 14." Without even thinking, I answer, "No, I'm not gonna take that low a price." We had $18,000 in the pot. If I had taken insurance at 14 to 1 at $2,000, that means I would have gotten $28,000, so I would be winner to the pot anyhow. But I said no—and she caught a 5 on the end!

When you stop to think about it, insurance sometimes is well worth taking. Anytime you can get big odds, you probably should take it because, as Murphy's Law goes, "Anything that can go wrong will go wrong.

"Just ask me!

Had I taken insurance in the Carey deal, I couldn't have lost—either way. I would have won money, even though I would have had to give up a little bit. As it turned out I got nothing, and she won the whole pot.

STARTING HANDS

Now that we've covered some important concepts in pot-limit Omaha, let's move on to the types of starting hands you should be looking for. The best starting hands in pot-limit Omaha are:

Best Starting Hands in Pot-Limit Omaha

1. A-J-A-10 double suited and other premium high hands with aces and two connectors
2. A-A-K-K and other hands with aces and a big pair
3. Rundown hands that have four connecting cards
4. Three middle rundown cards with a pair
5. Two bare aces without connectors (for a minimum bet)
6. Two bare kings without connectors (for a minimum bet)

Big Pairs with Connectors

Although the computer says that the best hand to start with is A-K-A-K double suited, I disagree. In my opinion, the best starting hand is A-J-A-10 double suited. You can make only one straight with A-K-A-K, but you can make several straights with the A-J-A-10.

With the A-J-A-10 you still have the nut flush possibility. You don't get this hand very often, but when you do, you have a lot more possibilities than you do with the A-K-A-K.

Aces and a Big Pair

Like I said, I like A-J-A-10 double-suited better, but A-K-A-K is still a premium hand and you wouldn't mind it getting dealt all day long.

Rundown Hands

There are three categories of rundown hands, all of which are playable: middle rundowns, big rundowns and small rundowns.

MIDDLE RUNDOWN

BIG RUNDOWN

SMALL RUNDOWN

Rundown hands are major hands in pot-limit Omaha. If it's a small rundown hand such as 6-5-4-3, the only time being suited comes into play is when you're heads up. If you're playing a multiway pot where there's any action, someone usually has a bigger flush draw than you.

The rundowns are great pick-off hands if you've studied your opponents. Say there are two players in the pot and you know that one guy raises with aces and the other guy calls with big suited connectors. You have cards like 7-6-5-4 in your hand, and you say to yourself, "If the flop comes with any babies or middle cards, I've got it." So in this situation, you might play this type of hand. I do, and it's been very successful for me over the years.

On the other hand, you don't want to play heads up with these types of hands, so you wouldn't call a big raise with them against a single opponent. Suppose you flop two pair, you know the other guy has aces, and the board makes two pair that aren't your two pair. You're a goner. And you can really get involved with these types of hands.

The Small Rundowns

The small rundown hands are topped by the 7 on down: 7-6-5-4, 6-5-4-3, 6-5-5-4. I wouldn't suggest playing them in tournaments, but in side action, the small rundown hands can be profitable. If you're getting three-way action or more in a raised pot and you can put your opponents on big hands, calling a raise with a small rundown hand might take them off because you know you're the only one playing such a hand. In other words, you know your cards are live.

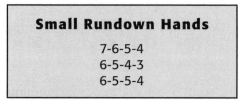

Small Rundown Hands

7-6-5-4
6-5-4-3
6-5-5-4

If you don't hit the flop, you throw the hand away. But a lot of times the flop will come with a small pair, and then you've made a set against an overpair. And quite often, you'll make a straight or two pair on the flop. If you've put someone on two aces, that's great.

Even if you call a small raise before the flop when you're getting a price to it multiway and you know where your opponents are at in the hand, you may well have a live hand— and a lot of times your opponents are trying to pick each other apart. Sure, you're spotting them the aces and the kings but you're getting a price for a live hand. Obviously, if the flop doesn't hit you, you're done with it but if it does hit you, you can bust some of these people.

Many times I'll play the small rundowns, knowing that I'm probably up against aces, when I really know where they're at. I know they have the best cards, but I'll take the chance to out-flop them with my live cards.

In tournament play you have less reason to speculate with these kinds of hands in raised pots because your opponents can put a lot of pressure on you. Therefore, you're less likely to want to play them in pot-limit tournaments than you are in ring games.

Three Middle Rundown Cards with a Pair

Another hand to play is three rundown cards with a pair, such as:

If you know you're up against a big pair and you flop one of your middle cards along with a straight draw, you'll have by far the best hand. If your opponents are playing big cards and your 8 flops, that 8 probably doesn't work with their hands, which means their straight possibilities probably aren't there either—unless they backdoor them. So almost any type of three-card rundown with a pair can be a good hand to play.

Notice that I said "almost." Forget about playing hands like 4-3-2-2. The danger is in set-over-set situations, and you usually can't flop the nut straight with a hand like that. If you play those little hands at all, it's usually from the blind in an unraised pot or from very late position for a minimum bet.

The Dangerous Dangler

The cardinal rule for rundown hands is this: Don't play hands that have a dangler in them. Don't let hands like Q-J-10-6 or K-Q-J-4 entice you into playing a pot.

A three-card rundown with a dangler:

A big pair with one connector and a dangler:

Suppose you have the above hand. You have three big cards working together and one oddball out there dangling off the roof. You usually don't play this hand. These types of hands can get you in a lot of trouble. Even if the dangler is suited, if it is not suited to an ace, it is still a dangler.

But in reality there are a lot of players who will call a minimum bet from late position with this hand.

Any hand with three or more gaps in it makes the fourth card a dangler. Don't play these hands. If you make a straight with a hand like this, it will never be the nuts. Playing a hand with a single gap and a pair—10-8-8-7, 9-9-7-6, or similar hands—is reasonable, but never play three-holers such as 10-9-5-4.

SINGLE GAP AND A PAIR

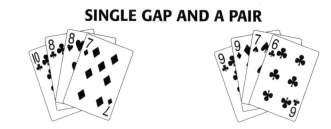

THREE GAPS

With two-gap hands—Q-Q-J-8, for example—you can sometimes make the nuts, but I'm not going to play this type of hand in a raised pot because it is marginal. I might play it against one man from out back for a raise if I know that the pot definitely will be heads-up. But I wouldn't play Q-Q-J-6 for a raise—there's that dangler again.

Two Bare Aces: No Connectors

Raising with aces, not getting any help on the flop, and then going broke to the hand is a big mistake. Some players will have $2,000 in front of them, get $1,000 in before the flop, see it come with 8-5-4, and move in with their aces. This is a bad move. If they get called, they're either beat or a huge dog. They could be against a set, a straight, two pair, or a huge wraparound drawing hand.

Suppose you have isolated an opponent in pot-limit Omaha and you know that he has aces. Sometimes, you will flop one pair, and even though you know that you're up against aces, you also realize that if you double-pair you'll win the pot. Of course, if the board pairs a card that isn't in your hand, the aces will take the pot with top two pair, but if it doesn't pair, you've got him. So, a lot of players will take off after somebody with aces if they just make one pair on the flop. I've done it a zillion times when I knew that my opponent had either aces or kings.

Two Bare Kings: No Connectors

Suppose you're dealt two kings double-suited. This is not a raising hand unless you're way around back (in a very late position). The reason it's not a raising hand is that if you get reraised you know that you're an underdog in the hand. But I see so many people make the mistake of raising with two kings, getting reraised, and calling the reraise.

What are you hoping to accomplish with this hand? You're just hoping to catch a king on the flop, but you're a dog to start with and, if you know that aces are out, the kings are in big trouble. Even if you have a pair of kings double-suited and you make the flush, if your opponent raises when you bet, you can be pretty sure that you're looking at the nut flush.

So in pot-limit Omaha, if an opponent is willing to put all his money in before the flop, a pair of kings is usually a piece of junk. In that case, you know that you're up against aces because any nit worth his salt is going to dog his hand unless he has aces.

Some players will raise limpers with K♠ K♦ 5♦ 4♥ from, say, sixth position with two players behind them. We don't recommend this play. If the raiser gets reraised he can use that hand for toilet paper! You should almost never raise with two kings and weak side cards against two limpers.

Remember that reraises in pot-limit Omaha are 90 percent aces, and if it's a good player reraising, it's aces with suits.

A good player may call with a hand such as A-A-9-8 with one or no suits, but he probably won't put all his money in before the flop unless his hand is much stronger than that.

But do you know where you might raise with two kings in pot-limit Omaha? In the little blind and the big blind—but if you do you're hoping that you don't get reraised. And you might raise from the button or very late position into the two blinds, with the idea of mucking the hand if either of them is willing to push it all in.

Trap Hands

You can lose a lot of money if you get caught with the second-best hand. Trap hands usually consist of kings and queens in raised pots. Queens double-suited, for example, can put you in a world of misery. King- or queen-high flush draws are other types of trap hands that are even worse in pot-limit Omaha than in the limit version.

Position and Hand Selection

In pot-limit Omaha, position isn't as important before the flop as starting hand selection. However, once the flop is out there, position is important.

The thing that is really important about position is this: If you play a hand, can you stand a raise with it? Whether or not people are willing to stand a raise with hands such as medium rundowns—8-7-6-5, for example—dictates whether they will play those types of hands from up front. I'm willing to stand a small raise with them so I'll play them. So long as you don't raise coming in and there's only a single raise behind you, that raise usually isn't so big that you can't call it.

In tournaments, position is somewhat more important. It allows you to put on a little more pressure because people can't go back into their pockets. But the value of your starting hands is still far more important than position.

Preflop Raising Alert

Practically no hand is worth raising preflop because people will know where you're at and play accordingly, but you won't know for sure where they're at. This is especially true in tournaments. If you're playing in a ring game, people will raise with aces because they're playing differently than they would play in tournaments and they will raise with a lot of different hands. With aces, you're always trying to narrow it down to one other player and yourself if you can.

When you raise, most players are already thinking that you have aces or something close to them, unless you're the type of player who regularly raises with rundowns. Of course, playing your aces when somebody has raised in front of you is a different story. Many times, you can put enough pressure on the pot to blow everybody away and sometimes even get the raiser to lay down his hand. If so, you can win it right there or at least get it heads up against the original raiser with what you know is the best hand.

If you insist on raising in this game, my advice is that the only hands worth raising are aces with connectors and suits or big connecting cards (A-K-Q-J). And even medium rundown hands are better hands to raise with than kings. If you put a man on aces, you don't want to have an ace in your hand: Aceless rundown hands such as K-Q-J-10 are what you want. You don't mind if he catches an ace on the flop because you need one.

With the K-Q-J-10, you'd like to see the flop come something like A-Q-10 because it makes a straight for you and if your opponent has pocket aces, you're likely to get a lot of action on the hand. Just remember that if you have an ace in your hand, your opponent started with two, and if one comes on the flop with the connectors that you're looking for, you'll make two aces and he'll make three of them.

You don't raise with kings, you don't raise with queens, and you don't raise with jacks in pot-limit Omaha. I'm not saying that you don't take a flop to these hands when you have connecting cards with them—but you don't raise with them. You're hoping to hit something on the flop but why put a lot of money in with them? If one overcard comes to your pair, you're often in trouble.

PLAYING ON THE FLOP

It's all in the flip of the flop. Once you see the flop, remember that you have seen seven of the nine cards from which you will make your final hand. Your big decisions are made on the flop, even more so than in the forms of two-card hold'em, because you have so much more information right there in front of you.

A lot more flops are seen in pot-limit Omaha and a lot fewer rivers are seen, unless all the money goes into the pot on the flop. With four cards in each player's hand, you'll find more multiway pots in Omaha than in hold'em, and in pot-limit, those multiway pots are usually three- or four-handed.

A lot of people will call a modest raise to see the flop and then fold on the flop. If three or four people have called a raise before the flop, the pot is pretty big and they would have to flop really big hands in order to continue. At that point, they can't play a marginal drawing hand.

Generally, when the river is seen in pot-limit Omaha, all the money is already in the pot—that is, if it's a big pot.

Top Two Pair

Generally speaking, if you have top two pair or bottom set and you get heavy action, you're a gone goose. You're up against either a gigantic drawing hand, which is a favorite, or a made hand, such as a higher set that has you beat. It's very easy to get away from bottom set in a multiway pot, but it's not so easy in a heads-up pot.

In hold'em, if you have Q-J and the board comes 7-8-9— giving you two overcards and a middle buster—you might take a shot with this hand. If you put your opponent on having a pair of one of the board cards, you might call with this hand since you have twenty ways to win—four tens, three jacks, and three queens—with two cards still to come. With those twenty wins you're approximately a 7 to 5 dog, which might be worth playing.

But in pot-limit Omaha, you'd never take a shot with it. In Omaha, there are so many backdoor possibilities that are unseen. A lot of times, you'll raise the pot with a hand like A-A-10-9 and you'll wind up winning the pot with the 10-9, not the aces. So often in Omaha, it isn't the primary cards that you win with, it's your secondary cards.

Flopping a Set

I've played a zillion Omaha hands where I flopped a set, another guy flopped a set, and a third player had a big draw against us, such as a straight or a flush draw. When that happens, a lot of times the sets are gone south for the winter—they're dead. This is another reason why the game is so treacherous, why you have to play so carefully, and why the better players will get the money in the long run. They can get away from hands that other people won't give up. They know to lay down that set or that 9-high straight when they can't improve or have no backdoor possibilities.

Ideally, you want to flop a good hand and have a draw that could improve it even further. For example, suppose you have 10♠ 10♣ 9♦ 8♠ and the flop comes 10♥ 7♠ 6♣.

YOU

FLOP

You couldn't get a bigger flop—you have the nut straight and top set. You could fill up and win if someone else has a lower set. If an opponents fills up, he won't win because you'll fill up higher. These hands seem like they're from Outer Mongolia, I know, but they come up all the time in Omaha.

Straights and Flushes

Suppose you flop the nut straight with no possibility of improving, and two of a suit also come on the flop. This can be a dangerous situation for you. You would like to have another draw when you flop a straight, such as a flush draw or a draw to an even higher straight. It's nice to make the nut straight on the end or on fourth street, where you can get enough money in to blow your opponents out of it. But on the flop, you can't get enough money in to do that, so you might want to play this hand softly.

If you bet into a certain type of player when he has a nut flush draw on the flop, he will empty his whole stack to draw to that flush. I don't think this is a good play on his part, although players sometimes do this as a semibluff to try to blow you away.

They might occasionally blow you away with a big raise, but there's less bluffing in pot-limit Omaha than you might think.

Most of the Time, Somebody's Peddling the Nuts

Pot-limit Omaha is a game in which you're peddling the nuts a great percentage of the time. If a good player is swinging at you in a pot, you can pretty well figure that he has the nuts, whatever the nuts can be at that point. So you take that into consideration. If you have a couple of draws to make the bigger nuts, then it's up to you whether you want to play or fold.

Unlike other games such as pot-limit hold'em in which, if you have the nuts, you try to trap. Iin pot-limit Omaha you peddle the nuts as fast as you can right on the flop. You don't give free cards unless you've flopped something gigantic, like quads. I'd hate to count how many times I've flopped the nut flush and given one card off only to see the board paired on the turn. If this happens, you have to slow down to a walk and pray that your opponent hasn't filled up.

It takes years and years to learn all the little nuances of play in this game. Every time you play it, you learn something different and the players are always going to be different and play in many different ways.

Bottom Two Pair

Bottom two pair in Omaha is absolutely nothing. You don't lead with it unless a player has reraised the pot and you put him on aces or kings. There's a big difference between doing that and making the mistake of leading against anything else.

Suppose you're playing against one man and you put him on kings or aces. If you flop bottom two pair, you can go after him because it is very likely that you have the best hand. But if you have top pair and bottom pair or bottom two pair in a multiway pot, you have to be very, very careful with them. If you get any action, somebody usually has a set, top two pair, or top and bottom pair. In this situation, those bottom two pair are bad cards. If you fill up, you think you have a hand but you don't have anything—somebody usually has a bigger full house.

Bluffing

There are some times when you can bluff in pot-limit Omaha. Specifically, if you have the lone ace of spades in your hand and three spades hit on the flop, you know that nobody can have the nut flush. Sometimes you can run people off in this situation. While that's true, you'd better try that play against good players. Never try it against a weak player, because he will call you with that small flush for all your money.

Everybody knows the lone ace play when three of a suit are on the board. So a lot of times good players will chop you off when you try to make the play, and other times they will fold. But bad players never throw anything away. If they have a flush, they're calling. Also, you shouldn't overwork this play against good players. And if you do win the pot with that lone ace, you never show it—just throw your cards away. Don't let them know that you even know the play. You never want to show a hand if you don't have to.

When I won the pot-limit Omaha title at the Four Queens, it was down to Slim and me. I had a jack-high flush, and I knew that I had the best hand. When three clubs came on the flop, Slim moved in. I beat him into the pot with my flush. He had a 10-high flush, but I knew I had the best hand; my instincts told me so. I wouldn't make that play very often, but Slim has a way of talking—he talks one way when he has a hand and he talks another way when his hand is weaker. And you know, he's talking all the time, so you just have to pick up on the intonation of his voice and what he's saying. In the two pots that he had beaten Mansour Matloubi and Mike Sexton for all their money, I knew that Slim had a hand. I wasn't in the pot but I knew he had the hand. And I used that information to beat him when we got heads-up.

It all goes back to knowing your opponents. Doyle Brunson talks about the importance of having recall. In his opinion, the thing that makes a poker player great is his ability to recall, maybe not what that exact player has done, but what that overall class of players has done in past situations. But while Doyle works with classes of players, I work with individual players. I have total recall when it comes to players and situations. I don't know why I have that ability; I forget lots of things. I've even forgotten my book-writing appointments while on the golf course. But I don't forget how a person plays.

One day I was playing in a $40/$80 game and this guy that I'd never seen play before played his hand exactly the same way every time. He check-raised on the flop every time he had a hand. So I tell myself, "I'm never gonna bet when this guy's in the pot with me. I'll never bet without having a huge hand because I know he's gonna raise me." You use that kind of information to your advantage.

I've been in situations with Tom where I could have told you exactly which two cards he had.

"Yes," Tom says, "but I've also known when you were making a move at me and I called you. The classic example was at a recent Commerce hold'em tournament. I raised with A-J and you put all your money in on a reraise. I thought about it for less than two seconds and called because I knew you were making a play. As it turns out, you had a suited K-J, caught runner-runner to make a flush, and broke me! But I was dead right. I had you exactly where I wanted you. I was dead right and got dead broke!"

When There's Action on the Flop

If you get action on the flop, keep in mind that a lot of the cards you need to make your hand might be gone already. In a nine-handed Omaha game, thirty-six cards are out before the flop, and one card is burned making thirty-seven cards out. That leaves fifteen cards in play, which you count as sixteen because the burn is a random card. A lot of the cards you need to make your hand are already out and you have to take that into consideration. For this reason, I believe the game should be played seven-handed so that there's more of a deck to play with.

Now let's take a look at a situation in which you've raised before the flop with a premium hand and you don't catch the flop that you had hoped for.

You've started with the best hand possible, A-A-J-10 double-suited:

There's a lot of money in the pot, and the flop comes:

FLOP

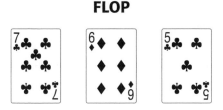

What do you do? You're gone—you fold.

Now suppose the flop comes:

FLOP

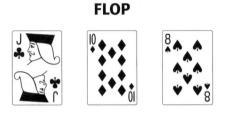

You have top two pair, but you don't have a straight draw. How do you play this hand?

Carefully!

You've raised before the flop, but if you get any action, somebody might already have the straight, and somebody else might have a set. The top two pair isn't necessarily the best hand. You're not as worried about somebody having a K-Q draw at the top straight because you have two of their straight cards with your two aces. Because of your preflop raise, these people are giving you credit for having aces. If they play the hand, the idea that you have two aces has gone through their mind and they know that two of their outs are gone, so the K-Q might not be the hand that's being played against you.

The Idiot End of the Straight

Now let's say that you have 7-7-6-4 in your hand and the flop comes with 9-8-2. You never draw to this hand. If four fives remain in the deck, all you're hoping to do is catch one of them. If a 10 comes on the turn, you're usually up against a top-end straight. You don't draw to the idiot end of the straight. Have I ever done it? Yes, I have. And have I won big pots with it? Yes, but I was lucky. Very lucky! And have I lost with it? Yes, I have.

You have to know your own skill level and who you're playing against, because you can get absolutely murdered in pot-limit Omaha.

The Wraparound Hands

I recently stood a raise in a cash game with 9-9-8-7. The board came 7-6-2 and no suits.

T.J.

FLOP

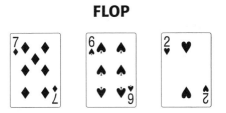

A guy led off with a decent bet and I called him. All I had was an open-end straight, but I had the top end of it and the top pair, so it looked like I might win the pot if I could double-pair. And if I could make the straight on either end, I could win the pot. Plus, I knew my opponent was a pretty loose player, so I called, made the straight on the turn, and won a nice pot. But if I'd gotten big action in this hand, I probably wouldn't have played it because all I had was an open-end straight draw, not a wraparound.

Having a wraparound makes a big difference. Say the flop comes 10-7-2 and you have J-9-8-6 in your hand. That's a complete wrap, meaning you can catch a card on either end or in the middle and make your hand.

Now suppose the flop comes J-10-2 and you have K-Q-9-8. You can catch any card on either end, or one of your own cards, to make your hand. We call it "Maine to Spain," and it's a big, *big* hand.

Inside and Outside Wraps

Suppose the flop comes with A-10-4 and you have K-Q-J-9 in your hand. You have an **inside wrap**. Or if you have a K-Q-9-6 and the flop comes J-10-4, you have a three-card **outside wrap**.

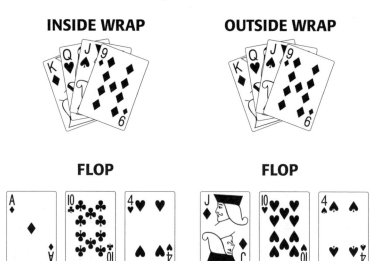

INSIDE WRAP	OUTSIDE WRAP

FLOP	FLOP

If you get a big draw like this on the flop are you going to push it? Sometimes. It depends on what you're up against. A lot of times, if you know by his actions that a player has top set and you don't catch your card on fourth street, you're done with it. You might be a favorite on the flop, but if you miss it on the turn, you're a dog.

A lot of players will play that hand very aggressively on the flop and commit themselves so they can't be blown out if they don't make it on fourth street. Other players might make a pot-sized bet that will double the price that it costs other players to go for their draws. If somebody comes out on fourth street with a big bet and you haven't made it, you have to make a decision: "Do I want to try to make this hand or not?" If you haven't led to this hand or raised—meaning you don't have a lot of money invested in the hand—you can get away from it now at a fairly cheap price. You have to give yourself that option, and that's why you often don't lead with this hand.

A complete wrap with no suits on the board—that's a hand you'll go to war with quite often. Many times, you will commit enough money on the flop to ensure that you're going to see two cards. Sometimes, it all depends on how you're running and other factors like that. It shouldn't matter, but somehow it does. Just because you've lost five hands in a row doesn't mean that you're going to lose the sixth one. The odds on the sixth hand are the same as they were on the first one.

Logically, what's the difference if you've lost five hands in a row? If you've played them right and you didn't get there, so what? Whatever the odds are of your making the sixth hand, they are still intact.

Slowplaying

Is there a correct time to slowplay a big hand from up front or try a check-raise? Usually not. You can't give free cards in Omaha because there are too many ways of making a hand.

I think that it's a huge mistake to give free cards. When players who have been playing a lot of pot-limit hold'em move to pot-limit Omaha, you'll see them making the mistake of using slowplay tactics to try to trap people. In Omaha, there are so many people holding backdoor hands who wouldn't call the flop if you bet. But you don't bet and suddenly they catch a magic card that gives them a flush draw, a straight draw, a set, or this and that, so now they're going to play.

Therefore, if the flop comes with a 5-4-3 and you have 9-8-7-6, you are not going to slowplay it on the flop. You're better off firing and hoping that someone has enough of a hand to come after you. If they raise you and there are no suits on board, you like that.

However, I'd feel a lot better doing it with the nut flush than with a straight. We've already told you that if you flop the nut straight and there's a lot of action, you can throw the hand away, and that's why this example works better with the nut flush. If you check your nut flush and the board pairs, you can be in a lot of trouble. You might not be, but you would play it as though you were.

Once the boards pairs and you have a straight or flush, you can't play with any real confidence.

What's really interesting about this game is that if there's any action at all, good players will throw their hands away when they flop a set and the flop also comes with three of a suit. But the weaker players know only that they've flopped a set.

"I've got a set," they say to themselves, "and I don't care if the other guy has a flush. I'm gonna pair this hand and beat him."

And sometimes they do, but in the long run they're going to lose their money.

When You Get It, Bet It!

As a general rule, if you flop the nut flush, you bet the nut flush. You don't slowplay; you play very straightforwardly. But that's not a cut-and-dried rule. Let me tell you why: There are players who play two pair like they are four of a kind. If you are in a game with a player like this and you know that he will bet two pair or a set on the flop with three of a suit on the board, you might slowplay against him. You might just flat call. You're taking a chance that the board won't pair, but you know that you're playing against a very aggressive player who will bet again and commit himself to the pot.

There are some other hands you can consider slowplaying. If you flop the top set with the nut flush draw, you might slowplay. However, keep in mind that sometimes leading with those hands creates bigger pots. Suppose somebody else bets into you when you have top set and the nut flush draw on the flop. You're not going to raise him right there.

For example, say that you have a K-Q-Q-J with one suit and the flop comes Q-10-9. You have top set and the straight. This is a good example of when you can give a free card, provided there isn't a suit out there.

But what if it also comes with two of your suit? Then you'd have the nut straight but only a second-nut flush draw. What should you do? Well, Columbus took a chance, and I might, too! This is the type of hand that if someone bets into you, you might smooth call because you have an extra out.

A lot of times, if a player flops two pair or a set when the flop comes with three of a suit, he'll lead out to see if his hand is any good. If he gets called, he'll often shut down. Then you'll have to bet it on fourth street and leave it up to him to decide whether or not he wants to go any further with it. If you have an opponent who's stuck and plowin,' he'll come. You hope that's the guy's who's in the pot with you.

The flop usually thins out the field, but you still see a lot of multiway pots. Many times, a ton of money goes in on the flop if any hands are out there—and in Omaha, there usually is something out there! But you'd better have the nuts or the nut draw if you call on the flop, and if you draw, you'd better be drawing to the nuts.

Suppose somebody bets in front of you, there are two hearts on the board, and you have the K♥ Q♥. Your question is, "Since one of my opponents might have the ace-high flush draw, why should I call?" But if you have the ace-high flush draw plus some other outs, that's a different story.

As I've said, I don't want to sacrifice all my chips on a one-type draw such as a flush draw in which I have nine outs twice—or eighteen total—if none of those cards are already gone. If I have an open-end straight draw, I have eight outs twice, or sixteen total. If I have a wraparound straight draw, I don't have much of a decision to make: I'm going to play.

To Play Past the Flop, Have Either the Boss Hand or a Draw to It

Either flop the nuts or have a draw to it. Remember that in Omaha players are peddling the nuts 90 percent of the time. They may not be peddling them in a heads-up situation—that's when the hands might be a little weaker—but in any multiway pot, somebody's drawing at the nuts if they don't already have it.

PLAYING ON THE TURN

The action usually thins down to two or three players on the turn, especially if there has been any action on the flop. It's very rare to see more than three players left if there has been a bet on the flop. Usually, if you make the nuts on the turn you bet it. And if anyone bets into you, you usually raise it.

Of course, there are occasions when you don't raise it. For example, when you make the nut full house or four of a kind, these hands are big enough that you can actually give a free card.

Straights and flushes usually are not big enough to give a free card because there's always the possibility that you're up against a set that your opponent might fill on the river. Say that you are on a draw and you make your hand on fourth street. Now you want to protect it. The pot will usually be big enough that you'll have a chance of doing exactly that with a pot-sized bet. If you make that bet with the nuts and someone does decide to call you, he has made a mistake, no matter what his draw is. If you have the nuts on fourth street, you're the favorite with one card to come, so you want to protect your hand at all costs.

Pot-Limit Omaha is Not a Free-Card Game

This is the cardinal rule of pot-limit Omaha. If you make your draw on the turn, you bet it. Just as you don't usually give free cards on the flop, you don't give them going into fifth street either. If you make it, bet it.

Don't forget that if you have called your opponent on the flop with a drawing hand, and the card that makes your hand comes on the turn, your opponent is going to be fearful that that card may have made your hand. So he's usually not going to bet it for you.

To put it another way, when you have the nuts, don't expect your opponent to bet it for you. Everybody is aware that the nuts can be out there, so when a card comes that can make them for someone, players will often shut down, even with fairly strong hands. You'll just have to do your own betting most of the time."

If your opponent is first to act and he led at the pot on the flop, he's not going to bet it for you on the turn. He's going to check to you. He might fold when you bet, or he might not. Remember that to start with he had something that he was leading at. Since he checked to you, he has to call only one bet to see the river, whereas if he had bet into you and you had raised, he would have had to call a whole lot more to see the last card. If it's an unraised pot that isn't too big, he might decide to try to beat you on the river. You welcome these types of players because they will have to draw out on you to beat you. Of course, in Omaha they do draw out on you a lot.

One other hand that I think you can give free cards in pot-limit Omaha is a straight that can't be improved. If you get action in front of you, are you going to raise with this hand right now? There might be two to a suit or a set out there. In this situation, just calling isn't the same as slowplaying the hand. You do it because you want to see what comes on fourth street before you get further involved. I'm just playing the hand slow, not slowplaying the hand.

When You Backdoor a Hand

Backdoor draws are ones that you don't recognize quite as often. Suppose the flop comes with two hearts and a club. You bet on the flop and your opponent calls—he's on a heart draw. Then on fourth street comes a second club. He may be double-suited in hearts and clubs and now has two flush draws, so he's probably going to play with you.

When you make a backdoor flush that isn't the nuts, it is less likely that the nut flush is out against you. A backdoor flush can be weaker, and it has much more value. That's another reason why this game can be so treacherous: A player can start off drawing at one hand and end up drawing at another hand. It's amazing how many times you'll see the flop come with two of a suit and wind up with three of the second suit on the board at the river.

If there's any action on fourth street, there's a far greater danger of someone backing into another draw—such as a flush that he wasn't originally drawing to—to go along with his primary draw that he called with on the flop. If you're the receiver of the runner-runner flush, you should often bet it even if it isn't the nuts.

Runner-runner has killed more Omaha games than anything else.

PLAYING ON THE RIVER

A lot of times there will be two or three players left on the river. You have to be careful if there are two or more people besides yourself contesting the pot. Just because there was only one club on the flop when you made your nut straight doesn't mean that someone can't make a flush on the river if it happens to come runner-runner clubs. It's far more likely to happen in an Omaha game than it is in a hold'em game. If you did flop the nut straight and two running clubs pop out, then you must play very cautiously at the river.

Of course, if you have the nuts, you want all nine players there with you.

There are times when bad things happen to good hands at the river. Let me tell you a story along this line. Bill Duarte is a very good player who we call "Boston Billy." I took a half of Bill in a real big ring game down at Oceanside that Phil Hellmuth, Tony Dee, and all those guys were playing. It got down to the three of them and Billy had the A♦ 10♦ 9♠ 8♠ in his hand. They made a little raise to come in and he called. The flop came with the 7♦ 6♣ 5♦. He flopped the stone joint three-handed, and he was drawing at the stone joint with the nut flush draw.

BILLY

FLOP

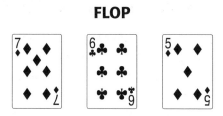

Tony Dee led off and made a big bet at the pot. Phil moved in, and Billy called for all his chips. This pot had almost $30,000 in it, and Phil was flat sizzlin.' Here are the hands that were out against Billy: Phil had the K♦ 3♦, the second-nut flush draw and nothing else. Tony had a jack-high flush draw in diamonds and the K♣ 7♣. He paired the 7 on the flop, which is what he took off betting with. Then all this money went in.

On fourth street the board pairs the 7 and now Tony has trip sevens. Phil's completely out of it, drawing dead. On fifth street comes the K♠.

BOARD

Tony caught a 7 on the turn to make trip sevens and a king on the end to make a full house! We lost this $30,000 pot where we had one man drawing dead and the other one drawing to two running cards for all the money. You can't get your money in any better than that. This just shows you what can happen in pot-limit games.

One interesting point to consider: With the 7-6-5 flop if the scenario had been slightly different—for example, if some players went to the center before it got to you and the board had two suited cards that weren't your suit—you would have had to give serious thought to passing this hand.

While that's true, you might consider playing it more often in a three-handed game than you would in a full ring game because with only three players in the game there are so many cards that aren't going to come out. In the shorthanded situation, more than half the deck is never going to be in play, but when you're playing in a full ring, most of the cards are out, and the hands that can be made are going to be easier to make. When there's a stub with half of the deck left, the cards that your opponents need to make their hands might never come into play because they might all be buried in the deck. I don't know if you've thought of it that way, but it's something to consider.

When You Miss on the River

Would you try a bluff at the pot at the river if you miss everything you've been drawing to? At this point the pot is usually pretty big, so you're talking about sacrificing a lot of money to bluff on the end. It's hard to think of a situation where I'd want to take the chance of losing a lot more money with a pot-sized bet. One of the top European players I've watched used to like to try bluffing on the end, but I've seen him get picked off so many times you wouldn't believe it. If they know you'll bluff, they will call you.

If you are going to try a bluff, you have to be a very strong player and know that your opponent also had been drawing and had missed his hand. We've all bluffed in our poker careers, but in the long run I think it's a bad idea to bluff at the river. I just can't see trying it unless you can absolutely put a man on a big draw that he has missed.

Why? Because a lot of money has been committed to the pot by then and most of these guys will call you so fast it'll make your head spin. When you're drawing, the other man usually isn't drawing. If he's a player, he has a hand.

The only time when you might be able to bluff at the river is when a card comes that will allow you to represent a hand. For example, say there were two flush cards on the flop and you've put your opponent on a set. If the third flush card comes at the river, you might take a shot at the pot. But you'd better know where you're at because you can get yourself called in a New York minute. A player might say to himself, "He's got the lone ace working and he's just trying to pull that lone-ace play on me," and then he'll call you. And if you're wrong in your evaluation of his hand, you'll lose all that money that you bet on the end. Sometimes you just have to suck it up and take a loss, take your medicine and move on to the next hand.

A lot of people think that the bluff is a big part of all poker games, but Omaha isn't really a bluffing game. Omaha is about peddling-the-nuts. There are certain situations in which you can bluff, but your win percentage on bluffs in Omaha will be a lot lower than it will be in hold'em. And in limit Omaha high, you can hardly ever run a successful bluff.

One more point here: Get in the habit of never showing your cards when you win a pot and haven't been called on the final bet.

Check-Raising on the End

Probably the only time you would ever check-raise at the river is when you're playing against a super-aggressive player. You have to know that he's going to bet at the river. Most of the time in Omaha a guy will shut down if he has been betting a big hand and fifth street damages him a little bit and makes better hands possible. In this case, you might as well bet and put him to the test, make him decide whether or not he wants to call the bet. If you're playing the hand for a check-raise, you will probably lose the money you would have won if you had bet on the end.

> A lot of people think that the bluff is a big part of all poker games, but Omaha isn't really a bluffing game. Omaha is about peddling-the-nuts.

Folding on the End

How often do you have to lay down a hand at the river? It isn't a good practice to lay it down at the river, but you might have been in there with a monster double-draw and miss everything at the end. In that case, you just lay it down—what else can you do? I can't think of any other reason why you'd go to the river and then throw away your hand.

A Bad Beat on the River

I was in a game at Tunica one weekend with a guy from Kentucky and we were playing $25/$50/$100 blinds. I had A-Q-Q-10 suited in hearts. The flop came Q-7-3 with two hearts. I had the nut flush draw and top set. I liked the hand.

T.J.

FLOP

I bet on the flop and he raised me. I raised him back and he called the reraise. On fourth street came an offsuit deuce. I took the lead. I had $27,000 in front of me before the hand started, and I put it all in the pot. He called me.

BOARD

  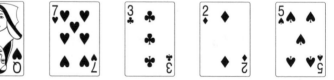

On fifth street came the 5♠, and he showed me a 7-high straight! He had a 6-4 in his hand. His flush draw was no good, my top set already had the pot won on the flop, and I ended up losing $27,000 on this one hand where he had three fives in the whole deck that he could win with.

I almost dropped out of my seat when that 5 came. I'll never forget it. The guy was on a suicide mission in this hand—he'd been on one most of the day, which is how he got stuck in the first place. His girlfriend would bring over these packets of $10,000 each, and he'd take two or three at a time from her and put them on the table. We were playing triple-draw lowball and pot-limit Omaha and I was $17,000 winner when this hand started. I could've gone to Lloyd's of London and gotten 100 to 1 on my hand after the flop. You can peddle the nuts but you can still lose.

LIMIT OMAHA
HIGH

LIMIT OMAHA HIGH

Tom McEvoy

Although limit Omaha high is an action game that many players enjoy, it has been eclipsed in interest by the even more action-packed split version, Omaha high-low. Some people believe that it is the volatility of limit Omaha high that has led to its decline in popularity, that too many players were going broke playing it, but I disagree. Limit Omaha high isn't spread at very high limits so people don't usually get broke playing the game. About the biggest game I've seen spread is $20/$40, and very few people are going to lose the ranch playing those limits.

What I'm saying is that limit Omaha high is not a bankroll buster; leave that distinction to pot-limit Omaha. People like games with lots of action and they often find a lot of excuses to play a ton of pots in limit Omaha high. They justify playing too many hands—a big mistake—and that is a major reason why this exciting action game has gained a certain degree of notoriety as a bankroll buster.

Position is less important in limit Omaha high than it is in hold'em because there are more playable hands. Blind stealing shouldn't even be in your repertoire. There is very little blind stealing in all forms of Omaha, but in limit Omaha high it is practically nonexistent. Because there are so many playable four-card combinations, you have to play pretty much on the merits of your hand. You have to show down a hand the vast majority of the time, so you must have a good starting hand, usually four connecting cards. You don't often think about bluffing, although occasions do come up when you can try it.

If you like to play Omaha high, and if you play it well, there is no reason why you cannot become a winner. In this chapter, T.J. and I discuss the strategies that we believe will take you to the winners' circle. Let's start off with seven of the most important concepts in limit Omaha high.

7 OF THE MOST IMPORTANT CONCEPTS IN LIMIT OMAHA HIGH

1. Players Are Usually Peddling the Nuts

In all forms of Omaha people are usually peddling the nuts. In limit Omaha high, you get the nuts paid off more often than you do in pot-limit Omaha because it only costs your opponents an extra bet or two to call. This is why there is even less bluffing in limit Omaha high.

There's less bluffing in all types of Omaha than in any other poker game. When there's a gigantic pot in Omaha it's usually hand against hand, or set against set, or hand against a giant draw that might be the favorite.

2. Chase Only When You're Drawing to the Nuts

Because they are usually getting pot odds for their draws, a lot of players chase, especially at the lower limits. Just remember that when you chase, you still need to be drawing to the nuts.

And you should have more than just one draw. You should have a multiway draw.

The point is that although you virtually always have proper pot odds, you still need to be drawing to the nuts or pretty close to it most of the time. In that way, limit Omaha high is similar to the split version where the cardinal rule is that after the flop, you must be drawing to the nuts in one direction or the other in order to continue with the hand.

3. Always Try to Have a Multiway Draw

When we say a **multiway draw**, we mean that if you're drawing to a straight, you're usually not in there drawing at an open-end straight. As in pot-limit, you need to have some sort of a wraparound: top wrap, middle wrap, or bottom wrap. Obviously, the only time you're going to be playing a bottom wrap is when you're putting your opponent on a set and you know that if you make the low-end straight it will be good.

You want to have more than one way to make your hand. An open-end straight draw is still just an open-end straight draw, no more.

4. Backdoor Hands Are Often Possible

Of course, there are a lot more backdoor hands possible in Omaha. A lot of times, your backdoor out will come in. Your three-straights and three-flushes that go with your flop hand sometimes make the difference between calling and folding. I'll give you an example of a hand that has a lot of backdoor value. Say you've flopped the top two pair with a straight draw and you also have two three-flushes. You're almost even money to pick up a flush draw on the turn card to go with your two pair. So if you have two pair, a straight draw, and two three-flushes, you have a pretty big hand. In that case, you can prepare to put a lot of heat on the pot.

Even better is flopping a set and a couple of three-flushes. Remember that if you backdoor a flush it usually won't be the nuts, but it still may be the best flush. It is less likely that you're going to run into a big flush, or any flush, when you backdoor one. Often, when you make a backdoor flush, it doesn't need to be as strong as it would if it were your primary draw—and that happens a lot.

In the pot-limit version I know a top player who often will peel off a card just to pick up a draw, but that's usually not a good idea unless you have something else to go with it. If you have two three-flushes, they should not influence your play. If they come, they come, but you certainly shouldn't consider them in the way you play the hand. You're not going with the hand on the basis of one or two three-flushes. Three-flushes do add value to your hand, but you must have a two-pair hand, a set, or a big wraparound in addition to them.

5. Playing Aggressively Has Merit

In limit Omaha high, if someone leads into you on the flop and you raise to build the pot, sometimes your opponent will fold and sometimes he will call. But suppose he reraises. Does the reraise mean that he has you beat? That's where your poker skills come in. Whether or not he actually has you beat, you still play it—but that's limit Omaha.

You can play more aggressively in the limit game than in the pot-limit version. And you should play more aggressively to maximize your win. In pot-limit you have to slow down a little because the pots get so big. You never have to worry about maximizing your bets because they're going to be maximized.

The biggest difference between pot-limit Omaha and limit Omaha high is that you shouldn't get broke on one hand in the limit game. But a lot of times players will take chances in limit games. They'll call a couple of bets with big pairs and no connectors. If the big pair in their hand is higher than anything on the board, they will call a bet. Then they hope to hit their overpair on the turn and win the pot, which I think is a foolish play, but they do it.

6. Playing Straights Correctly is Important

In limit Omaha high, you will play situations that you would never consider playing in pot-limit Omaha. You will stand raises with more borderline hands in limit than you ever will in pot-limit. If you flop the nut straight in limit Omaha high, you'll play it even if there are two suited cards along with it, but in pot-limit you might find yourself folding it on the flop if there's any action.

The point is that in limit Omaha high you'll play your nut straight on the flop even with two suited cards on the board because it's only costing you one unit at a time. But in pot-limit Omaha it can cost you your whole stack once there's money in the pot. Therefore, hand selection on the flop is one of the basic differences between the two games.

7. Top and Bottom Pair Can Be Dangerous

Flopping top and bottom pair can be fine if you're against one person, but it's really not the hand to be betting against more than one opponent in Omaha. And you definitely don't want to be playing the bottom two pair. The bottom two pair in any form of Omaha is death and destruction.

Suppose you're playing in a limit Omaha high game with that dangler hand, the K-Q-J-2, and the flop comes K-8-2. You've flopped kings and deuces, top and bottom pair. If someone bets, you call, and there's a raise behind you, there's a pretty good chance you're up against three of a kind or kings and eights, at the least. You're in trouble.

YOU

FLOP

Even if you're playing a hand with a pair in it and flop bottom set, you'd better be prepared to throw it away against any action.

This is why the small pairs can get you into a world of hurt when you flop a set to them. There are a lot more sets out in Omaha than in other games. Set over set, which is relatively rare in hold'em, is a common occurrence in Omaha games.

Now let's move to a discussion of the best starting hands for limit Omaha high.

STARTING HANDS IN OMAHA HIGH

In limit Omaha you play more hands and stand more one-bet raises than you do in pot-limit Omaha. Players will play more hands in limit Omaha high because it will only cost them one or two bets, whereas in pot-limit it could cost their entire stacks. So, there are more players per hand in limit

Omaha than in pot-limit. On fourth street, three, four or five players may still be in the hand.

In computer rankings of Omaha high hands, where your percentage of wins with one particular hand is computed against that of other hands, A-A-K-K double-suited ranks as the best possible starting hand. Not everyone agrees with the computer. T.J. is one of them: "I thoroughly disagree with the computer on that one. I think the best possible hand you can start with in Omaha high is A-A-J-10 double-suited," T.J. says.

You can make more straights with this hand than you can with A-A-K-K double-suited, T.J. points out. Naturally, you can't make three kings with the A-A-J-10 but the only thing that having two kings in your hand does for you is give you the possibility of making three or possibly four kings. The A-A-J-10 nullifies the power of the kings by having that many more hands you can draw to that will be nut hands if you make them.

T.J.

FLOP 1   **FLOP 2**

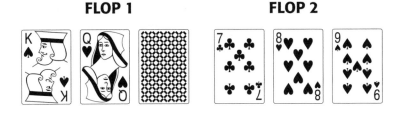

FLOP 3

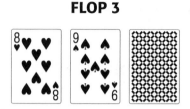

If the flop comes with a K-Q (Flop 1), you have a wraparound straight draw and an overpair. If it comes 7-8-9 (Flop 2), you have the nuts with the J-10. If it comes with an 8-9 (Flop 3), you have a great top-wrap with the aces also working. In fact, every straight that you can make with the J-10 and the two aces are nut hands. And you still have the possibility of making the nut flush in either of your suits.

Plus, look at what happens when the flop comes J-J-x (Flop 4) or 10-10-x (Flop 5).

FLOP 4	**FLOP 5**

You have top set with top kicker working for you and an overpair. A lot of times, a small pair will come on the board, and then you have a chance of winning the pot with aces-up. With a flop such as 7-7-2 (Flop 6), for example, you might win with aces and sevens.

FLOP 6

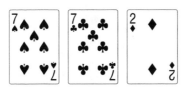

Now let's discuss the specific types of starting hands that we recommend playing high Omaha. The starting hands for limit Omaha high and pot-limit Omaha are basically the same. Let's take another look at them:

BIG PAIRS WITH CONNECTORS

ACES AND A BIG PAIR

THE BIG RUNDOWNS

THE MIDDLE RUNDOWNS

THE SMALL RUNDOWNS

THREE MIDDLE RUNDOWN CARDS WITH A PAIR

The main difference between pot-limit Omaha and limit Omaha high is not the hands that you start with, but how many of them you play. In pot-limit, you can play one hand in an hour and make three or four times the chips you had when you started. In limit, you have to win a lot of hands to stay alive.

In limit Omaha high, you play the small rundowns more often and deeper into the hand. You can also play them up front. Examples of these hands, four connectors or a pair with connectors, are 4-5-5-6, 4-5-6-7, 4-5-6-6, 5-6-7-7, and 6-7-8-8.

Since there are more multiway pots in Omaha high, you can play more rundown hands. But playing marginal hands in any poker game is just plain dumb. And I repeat: Don't play hands with danglers.

Playing Marginal Hands and Danglers Can Break You

The worst dangler in the world is A-K-Q-7. It's similar to razz when you start with a paint in the hole and two premium low cards (ace through 5), or **perfects**, against a player with three perfects. Then you both catch perfect on fourth street, giving you three perfects and your opponent four. Here, you're taking much the worse of it.

Now back to Omaha. If you have A-K-Q-2, at least you can make a straight with the deuce. It might not be the nuts, but you can make it. Of course, you're still in danger because of that dangler. Suppose you play A-K-Q-2 and the flop comes A-7-2. Now you have top and bottom pair, but what are you going to do with it? If somebody bets, you might be up against an A-7 or a set. You can get in a lot of trouble with that dangler.

It is common knowledge that hands like K♣ Q♣ 8♦ 7♦ are not good Omaha hands, but people sometimes play these types of hands, which are like two separate hold'em hands. You want four cards that connect in some fashion, even if there is a gap. For example, J♣ 9♥ 9♣ 7♥ has gaps and isn't that strong a hand, but there are conditions under which I might play it—for example, in an unraised pot, when there's multiway action and I'm on the button, or in the small blind for one-half a bet.

WORKING CARDS SOMETIMES PLAYABLE

Being double-suited adds a little bit of value to the hand, although I wouldn't be too excited about the flushes that I could make. But at least these are working cards.

Now a hand like J♣ 9♣ 8♥ 3♥?

No thank you. It's a piece of garbage, and yet people play hands like that.

GARBAGE HAND

Although the standard starting hands in limit Omaha high are similar to those in pot-limit Omaha, the main difference is that you can go farther with the hands and take more chances with them in limit. Also, you may be more willing to come into the pot from first position with a hand like 4-5-6-7 in limit Omaha high than in pot-limit, where you know how many other people will be coming into the pot and pounding you.

Middle Connectors

I might be more willing to mix it up with middle or small connectors from early position in the limit game. I totally agree with T.J.'s philosophy that in pot-limit, you can play those cards for a small raise from late position because you're getting a big price and you have a chance to take somebody off who will gamble with you with just overpairs. But in limit games, there is even more reason to play them, because there are so many more multiway pots in which you'll be getting the proper odds. You can play any four connecting cards if you can see the flop cheap—any four connectors, that is, except the low wheel cards (2-3-4-5). In pot-limit players force most of their opponents out of the pot with big preflop betting, but in limit Omaha high that isn't the case.

We have said that you take more chances in limit Omaha.

Let's say that somebody raises—raised pots are very common in the limit game—and I have 3-4-5-6 in my hand. I'm probably going to play this hand in the limit game, whereas in pot-limit I'll play it only once in a while, say in a side game when I'm going to try to knock somebody off who has a lot of chips. In limit I'll play this hand because it costs only a certain amount of money every time. It doesn't cost you anymore to play that hand than it does to play a pair of aces. Then if you flop to it, you'll take somebody off who is playing a big pair.

In limit Omaha high, if a player has two aces and the flop comes 9-7-2, which could give somebody a wraparound, that player is liable to lead at the pot. If you had 10-8-7-6 in your hand, he's in trouble. That's why you play these types of hands every now and then in limit, while you can't always play them in pot-limit.

T.J. thinks you should always have suits in Omaha, even in limit games. But you don't necessarily want to have 3-4-5-6 with suits because if two flush cards come out on the flop, what are you going to do? Try to draw to a 6-high flush? You're only hoping to make a straight with a low rundown hand like that.

Also, any four connecting cards are usually worth calling a raise with. Again, in limit you can't get broke to the hand, whereas in pot-limit you can. In any form of big-bet poker, you can often distort the pot odds to make the drawing price unprofitable, but in limit games you can't. These wraparound straight draws against overpairs are huge favorites with two cards to come and yet players still get married to their aces in Omaha, just like they do in most other games.

If you're watching your opponents and learning how they're playing, seeing what they're showing down, the kinds of hands they play, you'll know what kinds of hands they raise with. If you know that a guy only raises with aces, aces suited, or kings, you're going to play the small rundowns such as 4-5-6-7 against him because you're trying to take him off the aces. If you don't flop to it, the hand's easy to get away from.

Raising Hands

Raising hands include a big rundown, such as A-K-Q-J double-suited or at least single-suited, and a big pair with connectors, such as K-J-K-10, with at least one suit. You also can raise with rundowns such as a J-10-9-8 or a Q-J-10-9 if you are in late position and are the first one in the pot.

When you have big pot odds in limit Omaha high, your primary reason to raise before the flop is to build the pot. You want people who are willing to gamble even though, many times, you may have to abandon your big cards on the flop. Also, you can raise from any position to build a pot because you can't get broke by raising.

Your raise might force some of the marginal holdings out, of course, but if it's a wide open game and they'll gamble with you, you want to make them take the worst of it before the flop, while you still have the best of it. You want to make your opponents who are drawing to worse starting hands put in their money up front. It is always correct to raise to try to build the pot under these game conditions.

PLAYING ON THE FLOP

Obviously, if you don't hit anything on the flop, you fold the hand. The kinds of draws you want to flop are those in which you have more than one draw to a hand that you think will win the pot. When I have a hand that gets there on the flop, the only consideration in my mind is, "How do I maximize my profit?" I don't want to give a free card if it is likely to beat me.

If I'm first to act, the question is, "Do I think my opponents will bet if I check?" When a scary flop or a scare card comes, a lot of players may not want to bet but they will call you if you bet. You have to sense this type of thing. So I will play my hand in a straightforward fashion most of the time. I'm not going to try the fancy check-raise nearly as often as I might in hold'em. I'm just going to fire away at my opponents.

If I think that I have the best hand, especially if I think that one of my opponents has a set and will probably draw to try to fill up, why give him a free card? Suppose I am on a flush draw, for example, and the obvious flush card comes on the turn. If I check and my opponent has a set, he's most likely going to check as well, so it makes no sense to check to him.

Also, you usually have more than one opponent in limit Omaha high. If several of the players are even halfway decent, they will be afraid of that flush card, so you have to bet your own hand, rather than hope that someone else will bet it for you. You have to do your own dirty work. I don't ask others to do something that I am not prepared to do myself, unless it's housework—then I'm willing to pay.

Giving Free Cards

The only time you should give free cards is when you are holding the nuts and can't be drawn out on. When it comes to flopping quads, you should go right ahead and bet them because people are usually going to call anyway. Of course, not everything is a hard and fast rule. Whether or not I would slowplay the quads depends on the texture of the flop. I might lean less toward slowplaying them if, for example, I have a pair of queens and the flop comes K-Q-Q. I'm more likely to bet the queens in that situation, especially if the king is suited to one of the queens. That way, people would at least have a reason to play with me because they'll be drawing to flushes or straights—drawing dead, of course, unless they have a royal flush draw. But if it comes a rainbow flop with three mixed suits and a non-connecting card—Q-Q-4, for example—then I think you almost have to check at least once to allow someone to try to catch something.

You should also consider how likely it is that your opponents will draw dead. Some players who are really nutted up are not going to draw to a nut flush when the board has already paired. In this case, you have to check at least once to create some doubt in their minds that you have a big hand. But if you're playing with people who will gamble, which is what you want, then go ahead and fire away.

One nice thing about betting the nuts in any form of poker, Omaha in particular, is that when you fire right out with it, very seldom do your opponents give you credit for the nuts. The texture of the game, as well as the texture of the flop, dictates a lot of your betting strategy.

Free Cards in Tournaments

In tournaments it's different. People who give free cards in tournaments are just asking to get slaughtered. The only hands worth checking in a tournament are the mortal nuts or close to it. But if your opponents are willing to mix it up and it looks like there are drawing possibilities, you don't even check the absolute nuts.

In the pot-limit chapter, we mentioned giving free cards with a straight that can't be improved, because if you get action in front of you, it might mean that two to a suit or a set is out there. We can relate this idea to limit Omaha high. Sometimes, for example, you and an opponent each have the opportunity to draw out on the other. He could have a set to go with his nut straight, or maybe you have a flush draw to go with your nut straight.

This type of thing comes up frequently in pot-limit, and players have thrown away what they knew was the nuts at the moment because they knew their opponent also had the nuts plus a freeroll against them. But in limit Omaha high if I have the nuts at the moment or if I think my hand might be vulnerable—even if I suspect that someone else also has the nuts—I still may put in a raise to try to narrow the field.

Now, if my opponent plays back at me, we both have the nuts, and I know he's a reasonable player, I'll just call. This happens most often when you both have the nut straight with no other draws to improve the hand. When that occurs, I have to slow down and ask myself, "What is he raising me with? I've tested him once and narrowed the field."

If I'm in front position and have the nut straight, it might go this way: I bet it, a guy raises after me, and I reraise to narrow the field of players yet to act between him and me—as long as I have the nuts, that is. Or if I think my opponent and I both have the nuts, but I also have a freeroll against him, I will most likely reraise. If he's flopped the nuts, he can't go anywhere in the limit version. Although great pot-limit players will occasionally lay down the nuts on the flop, there is less reason to do this in limit Omaha because you can't get broke to the hand.

In all forms of Omaha the nut hand is out there more often than in other poker games. This almost always is true where straights are concerned, and the nut straight can easily be out in more than one hand.

Here is an example of slowplaying in a tournament situation: Suppose you have an A-K in hold'em and the flop comes A-A-10. You check and it's checked all around. Then on the turn comes a jack. Now what are you going to do? Someone may have a K-Q in his hand and make the nut straight on the turn because you gave him a free card on the flop.

Or suppose someone has a small pocket pair—sixes, for example. A red 6 comes on the turn, which looks like an innocent card. Because you gave that little pair a free card on the flop, he now has a full house and you're still drawing.

Although this example comes from a hold'em game, the lesson applies to Omaha, because the same problem is even more likely to arise in Omaha, where people have four cards to start with and usually have more starting pairs. So if you have flopped the nuts or close to it, you don't want to give free cards that could allow your opponents to beat you. You're in a spot in which your opponent may be able to beat you, but he can't call a bet anyway unless he can beat you. So it makes no sense to give him a free card because he can't give you any action anyway unless he has caught a magic card.

Always Make the Play That Will Maximize Your Profit

You want to make the play that you believe will maximize the money that you can make on that hand. For that reason, you can play more aggressively in limit Omaha high because very often that aggressiveness will maximize your profit.

Actually, in limit Omaha high there usually is less reason to disguise the strength of your hand. People will find excuses to get in the pot anyway, so what you want to do is make people pay to draw against you, as long as you think you have the best of it. If you have such a big draw that you're a favorite over even a set, you should charge forward.

Be Careful with Decision Hands

While playing Omaha, you're going to run into a lot of the decision hands that we discussed in the general strategy section of this book. In limit Omaha high, these decision hands are usually the middle rundown hands. You have to decide whether you want to get involved with them or not, which partly depends on how well you know your opponents. If they're playing high cards all the time and they're playing solid, you might take them off with a middle rundown hand. You have to decide whether you want to try that.

Another time that you run into a decision situation is when you have to determine whether or not your king- or queen-high flush is good enough to win. The good players can tell from the way the betting is going, and who's doing the betting, when it's okay to draw to these hands.

PLAYING ON THE TURN

Suppose you call the flop with a flush draw, but on the turn you miss it. Now what do you do? If you can get a free card, that's great, but even if you don't, you still can call a single bet if you are drawing to the nuts. What you don't want to do is get caught in the middle between two people who are at war with each other. If that is likely to happen, or if you call and then the war breaks out behind you with one card to come, you must abandon the hand unless you have other possibilities. If you have other draws to go with your flush draw that could also prove to be the best hand, then a lot of times you'll take the heat and continue with the hand.

Other types of draws might be big wraparounds or two-pair hands if your two pair are the top two pair. If you have top two pair and think that you're up against a set, you might call, hoping that you can pair up one of your top two cards.

For example, let's say that you have:

YOU

The flop comes:

FLOP

You know that there's a straight out there, but you have two pair and the nut flush draw. If two people start going to town or if a super tight player puts in a raise, you know that you're up against a made straight. But you have top two pair, the nut flush draw, and the ace with connectors, meaning you could catch a 10 to make the big straight and either win the pot or split it. If a nondescript card comes on the turn and you don't catch any of my outs, you're still covered, even if there's a raising war, and you will draw with one card to come. Of course, you would give it up if the board paired on the turn and it wasn't your pair—say if the board paired the jacks.

If all you have is the flush draw, your play should be different. This time, suppose your cards are:

YOU

A blank comes on the turn, so that the board reads:

TURN

Two people in front of you start going to war when the blank hits. In this case, you would abandon ship because all you have is the flush draw. However, if it costs you only one bet, you would call to see the river card because the pot usually is giving you a big enough price—approximately 4 to 1 with one card to come—to justify making the call for a single bet.

For a single bet—that's the key. If someone bets, you call, someone behind you raises, and then the original bettor reraises, you should give up.

But suppose there's a bet, you call, someone raises, and the original bettor just calls? Then you also would call. In other words, you might call a single bet twice but not a double bet once.

This example applies strictly to those occasions when you have only one way to make the hand and are not involved in a raising war. In addition, in this scenario you have some extra implied odds. Although you're a 4 to 1 dog, the pot usually is so big that if the flush card comes, people will grumble about how lucky you are but they'll often—if reluctantly—pay you off anyway. Or if they have made a flush, they might feel forced to pay it off on the end. And it gets even sweeter when an opponent with a flush draw that he thought was the best one bets into you and you raise him. If he's a bad enough player to bet less than the nut flush under these conditions, chances are that he's a bad enough player to pay off the raise, too!

When a Scare Card Comes on the Turn

Suppose you have drawn to your hand on the flop and on the turn comes a card so scary that you are no longer sure that you're drawing to the nuts. There's a lot of doubt in your mind.

For example, suppose you have:

YOU

The flop comes:

FLOP

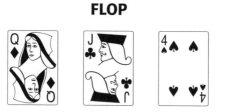

You've flopped top two pair and you have a straight draw, but you're only happy hitting an 8, a queen, or a jack. You're not happy hitting an ace, king, 10, or 9.

Now suppose a straight card comes on the turn, either a king or a 9 that can make a bigger straight than what you're drawing to. Take a look at the board:

BOARD

You're forced to check the hand because there's a good chance that you're already beat. You're reduced to possibly a six-out full house. Therefore, what was, on the flop, a reasonably strong hand that might have been worth gambling heavily with, becomes a very vulnerable hand on the turn. Plus, with two suited cards out there, if the other suited card comes and you don't have a flush draw, then what do you have? Zilch!

Or even worse, suppose you flopped a straight. Say you have a K-Q-Q-J, a decent starting hand, and the flop comes 10-9-8 with two of a suit.

YOU

FLOP

You flopped the nut straight and can even draw to a slightly higher straight if a jack comes. Then—boom! The third suited card hits. What do you have now? Nothing. You're done with it; you have to check-pass a hand that you were willing to push to the hilt on the flop.

Omaha high can be brutal! It's a cold, cruel world and this is a cold, cruel game. But it's not as cold and cruel as Omaha split, which is even more aggravating.

PLAYING ON THE RIVER

The river pretty much takes care of itself in limit Omaha high. There's a lot of drawing going on in this game, which means that the river card can drastically influence the results. You might have had the nuts all along, only to see it turn into a pile of manure at the end, when for example, the board pairs or the flush card gets there. Or you can draw to the nuts on the flop, make it on fourth street, and then an opponent makes the bigger nuts at the river. This happens a lot, and this is why Omaha players gnash their teeth into little stubs.

Now suppose that on the river you miss your hand and it looks like everybody else has missed, too. You're in an end position, everybody checks to you, and you're sitting there with two pair. Do you bet? Yes, if you have two pair that could win a showdown. You are less likely to bet if you think that you'll only get called if you're beat. But if you think that you have the best hand and might get a call, then you may very well bet.

A Steal Situation

What if I think that everybody was on a draw and they have all missed on the end, but I have missed as well? Occasionally, this is an opportunity to steal a pot. I'm not going to try to steal against four or five people, which is what I call Omaha suicide. But suppose a backdoor flush card hits, I have one or two opponents, and they both check to me, the last to act. Even though I was drawing to something else, they're afraid of this scare card that has come out there. I have nothing, but this could be an opportunity to steal.

I don't try to steal very often. I have to be in exactly the right situation against people who are either capable of laying down a hand and are a little bit on the tight side, or timid and freeze up every time a scare card hits. In this type of situation, I may very well bet with nothing on the end. If you try it yourself and get called, you might as well just turn your cards face down and throw them in the muck.

This means that someone with a baby flush or a low two-pair was too timid to bet it, but he was brave enough to call you. It pays to know these things about your opponents.

Don't try to bluff people who are timid but will check-call. Bluff people who will lay down a hand when they think that you might have made something. And don't even think of trying to bluff three or more players. Most of the time, I don't think about bluffing at all, but occasionally, I'll make this type of positional play at the pot against one or two opponents who I think are capable of laying down some hands that I wouldn't be able to beat in a legitimate showdown.

If I think that a bet has a negative expectation—that I probably will get called only if I am beat—I wouldn't bet, I would just show it down. And that happens a lot. Negative expectation bets come up more frequently in Omaha than they do in other games—like hold'em, for example. If you have a medium two-pair that may or may not be good because your opponents were on draws that didn't materialize, they can't call you, can they? But if one of them has a bigger two pair or a small set, he probably will check-call you. So you have to decide whether a bet on the end has a negative expectation.

TOURNAMENT PLAY

In limit Omaha high tournaments you have to be a little bit more conservative than you are in ring games to preserve your chips, unless you have a ton of chips. If I have a bunch of chips, I am more likely to mix it up with hands that are reasonable, though not great, holdings. This is when I'll take the four small connectors like 7-6-5-4 and raise from up front—when I have a lot of chips, everybody's short-stacked trying to hang on, and they don't want to mess with me.

Playing a Big Stack

When I have a big stack I'll pound away with hands that are less than premium but still have potential. And if I miss the flop, guess what? I'll just dump the hand. But I'll put some heat on them before the flop. And if I'm heads-up, I might put in one bet on the end even if I miss, because a lot of times my opponent is trying to preserve his chips so he can hang on and get to the pay table.

I admit it: I love being a bully. Unfortunately, the opportunities don't come up that often because it's difficult to accumulate a lot of chips. Dana Smith says that all accountants-turned-poker-players love to be bullies because they never had the chance to in their former jobs. That's correct. When I was in that 9-to-5 accounting job back in the '70s, I was the one who always got sand kicked in my face. Today in the poker world, I get the chance to kick a little sand of my own. The point is that when you have chips, you can open it up a little bit, but generally speaking, you don't open it up with trash hands.

There are times, however, that I do open it up with anything. I'll give you an example of one time when it didn't matter what my hole cards were. In the 1984 World Series of Poker, the first time a pot-limit hold'em event was staged, we were down to ten players. I had by far the biggest stack and there were several people just barely hanging on trying to make the last table because it only paid nine places, so I started just raising and playing every single hand.

More recently, a player from Michigan who has never before or since won a poker tournament did the same thing in the limit Omaha high tournament at the WSOP. He had accumulated a massive amount of chips so he began raising and playing every hand. He couldn't have had a hand every single time, but whenever somebody took a stand, he would show them a hand. He was super loose, super aggressive, and played every hand. I've never seen anything like it, and he bulldozed the entire table. This recreational player won a WSOP title just by using these aggressive tactics.

In the opening stages of the tournament, however, hand value is where it's at, until you can reach the point where you can be the bully. When you can't be the bully, you have to show down a hand most of the time. That's the nature of this game.

Playing a Dangler

There is one situation in a tournament when I might play a dreaded dangler hand, specifically when I am in the small blind. I really don't like danglers, but if I have three very decent cards and it's only going to cost me one-half a bet, this is one time when I am more willing to call with a dangler hand. In particular, if I have at least one nut-flush draw—one ace working—I will make the call.

I feel the same way if I'm in the big blind and all I have to call is a single raise. Here, it will cost me only one more bet when somebody raises, especially if there are several people already in the pot.

Suppose you have:

YOU

Not a very good hand, but the ace is suited, plus you have some slight straight chances and a minimal wheel chance. This is not a great hand, but under these conditions you would call a single raise with this hand. You're also prepared to play with extreme caution on the flop if it doesn't come just right for you. One nut flush and a couple of marginal straight possibilities should be your minimum requirements for a dangler hand in these circumstances.

The 1992 High Omaha Championship at the WSOP

When I won the limit Omaha title in 1992 against Berry Johnston, a shocking key hand came up while we were still in a full ring. There were some pretty good players at the last table—Frank Henderson, Brent Carter, Mel Judah, An Tran, Jim Boyd, Berry Johnston, and me. And that's why I value my victory so highly.

I was in the big blind in an unraised pot with a real junky looking hand—something like 6♥ 7♥ 8♣ Q♠—and I flopped a straight flush! Mel Judah, who had been playing ultra solid and was still trying to survive at that point, flopped the ace-high flush. I decided to lead with the straight flush rather than slowplay because I figured that if someone had the nut flush, the ace high, I might get some action. So I just fired at the pot. Judah called and everybody else passed. The turn card came a blank. I bet again, and he just called. The board didn't pair on the river, so again I bet and he just called.

When he turned over the ace-high flush, I said to him "How the hell could you just call with the nut flush?"

"I smelled a rat," he said. "What else could you have?"

This shows how smart he is. I think almost anybody else would've raised with that nut flush, but T.J. disagrees.

"If you have the nut flush and a man has led at you three times," T.J. says, "what hand are you going to give him if there's a straight flush possibility out there? I don't even know if I would have made the last call. It's hard to lay the nut flush down, but here you've made it and the other man's a player and he's doing the leading. What the hell can he have but the straight flush? A player of Tom's caliber, what's he going do? Lead out with the second- or third-nut flush three times in a row?"

Well, when Judah called me that last time, he did squirm in his chair a little bit! But he lost the absolute minimum on the hand and I was impressed with his play. The average player would've raised with that hand and lost a lot more to it.

I can see T.J.'s point, though. There were some very skilled players at that final table, and I don't know how the others would've played it. I only know how Mel played it.

Being Aggressive

"I won my first bracelet at the WSOP in limit Omaha high," T.J. says, "but I can't remember a single person who was at the final table! I just remember that it was the first time I'd ever played limit Omaha high in my entire life. And then my wife Joy and I went to Lafayette for the Cajun Cup and I won the same event there, too. I won those two tournaments back to back.

"Carl McKelvey and I played four and a half hours heads-up for the Cajun Cup championship. That was a battle. I guess the only reason that I won is because I was really aggressive. Anything that came out there, I was representing. And I wouldn't slow down; I was firing all the way. You know, if a guy's firing all the way, sometimes it's hard to call without having the nuts."

That's what happened when I played Berry Johnston heads-up in 1992 at the final table. He was definitely playing a little more conservatively than I was, and he had the chip lead most of the way. He made a couple of laydowns in situations where, if he'd called, I don't know if I could've taken the pot. But I represented what was out there and figured that he was drawing to something. Maybe he had two pair and a draw, but a flush card hit, so I bet it. A lot of times when you have the ace to the suit that's showing on the board, you can represent the nut flush because you know that no one else has it.

But you can only do that a few times. Any player will pick you right off if you try it too often. In limit Omaha high it's a little bit more risky because it only costs an opponent a single bet to call.

But back to the WSOP: Berry made laydowns in a couple of hands that allowed me to survive. At that tournament, I had the biggest comeback I've ever had at a World Series event. At one point, Berry had 90 percent of the chips. That's one reason I'm so proud of that victory. Berry has come back from a seemingly hopeless deficit to win as well. The point is that anyone—including you—can come back from near disaster and make a fine finish in a tournament. It just takes determination, timing, and a tiny bit of luck.

Playing Against Super Aggressive Opponents

Speaking of being aggressive in tournaments, a man who I know to be a really good tournament player told me that he can't figure out how to play against the Kamikaze pilots, guys that you know are going to represent everything on the flop every time. He says he doesn't know whether to play tight, loose, or just real solid.

The answer is that you just play your game. Let them play the way they want to play, but you always play your game. If your game is good enough, you're going to get the money. There isn't a poker player alive who doesn't lose, but in the long run the best players end up with the money.

You see, you can never judge poker by one game or one evening's play. A poker player judges himself by what he does for the year. One guy told me that he judges himself by the hides on his wall. If he has all the hides and you don't have any, he must be the better player.

**HIGH-LOW
HANDS
IN ACTION**

HIGH-LOW HANDS IN ACTION

T.J. Cloutier

YOUR HAND: A-A-2-3

This is the optimum hand you can be dealt in high-low. I usually would raise or reraise with this hand before the flop from a late position, even if the aces are single-suited or unsuited. If you flop two little cards, a flush draw, or top set, you have a huge hand. When you catch a good flop, play this hand strong. Why not? This is a limit game, so it can't cost you that much if you're on a draw and miss it. If your opponents don't bet, you bet.

But if you don't flop to it and there is any action in front of you, get rid of the hand. All you have is two aces, so what's the point in continuing? You couldn't ask for a better starting hand, but why lose money to it if the flop comes with a Q-J-10, 10-9-8, or something like that? If it comes with two high cards and one low card, you would need to catch runner-runner little cards to make the low. Against any action with that type of board, you can probably assume that somebody else already has a high hand, so your aces are no longer a factor.

DANGER FLOPS FOR A-A-2-3

Some high-low players make a big mistake when they start with a strong hand like this. If they catch only one little card on the flop with no other outs, they draw for a second low card on the turn. Sure enough, they catch that little card and then get hooked into drawing for a third one. Almost invariably the board rags off on the end or comes with a third high-straight card, and the chasers are out of the race.

YOUR HAND: A-2-3-4

A-2-3-4 is the second best Omaha high-low hand you can get. You'd like to have it suited to the ace, but even if it isn't suited, it's still a very strong hand. You can stand as many raises as you have to with this one.

Just remember that when you start off, you're only playing a low hand if the ace isn't suited. Obviously, you can make a wheel or a low straight that will scoop the pot, but keep in mind that you're usually playing for the low end of the pot only. For that reason, you don't want to make an initial raise with A-2-3-4 unsuited.

You can play back with it if you want to, but I would not make the first raise—let somebody else do it. A lot of times, putting in that first raise will tip off the strength of your hand, and why would you want to do that with a hand that might get paid big money on later?

If the ace is suited, this is a raising hand. Now you're thinking that you might be able to scoop the pot, which is the whole idea of Omaha high-low. The players who scoop the most pots are the ones who win the tournaments or the money in the side games.

Of course, you have a chance of scooping the pot even if the ace isn't suited, but you need a big, big flop to do it. Naturally, if the flop comes A-A-2, A-A-3, or A-A-4, you have a huge hand. In fact, the flop doesn't even need to come with two aces for you to have a big hand. If it comes with an A-2, A-3, or A-4, you have two pair, plus you're still drawing at the nut low. Even if the flop counterfeits two of your cards, you'll still have the boss low drawing hand.

YOUR HAND: K-K-Q-J

The K-K-Q-J double-suited is a powerful hand to play in late position. If the flop comes with three low cards, this hand is useless. If an ace hits the board and you haven't flopped any of your cards, you're also in deep trouble.

Suppose the flops comes:

FLOP

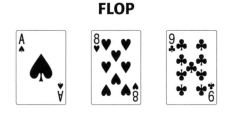

A 10 will make a straight for you, but that one lone ace on the board has you beaten right now, so just get rid of it. The hand looks powerful as hell to start with, but you still need the right flop to it.

Now suppose the flop comes 8-8-6.

FLOP

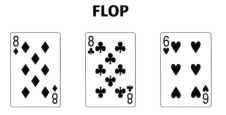

I've seen people call a bet on the flop with a big overpair against that type of flop, but I wouldn't do it. Why waste the money? You're calling with an overpair, trying to catch a two-outer twice. With two cards to come, you have a four-outer. And with two low cards on the flop, you're most likely up against two or more low draws. So even if you catch a king, you will have to split the pot if another unpaired low card comes.

YOUR HAND: 9-9-8-7

I will never play a 9-9-8-7 in Omaha high-low, unless I get stiffed in—I'm in the big blind and it's not raised—or it only costs me one more chip in the little blind. In Omaha high-low, play big cards and play little cards. And when I say "little cards," I don't mean that you should get stuck in there with a hand like 3-4-5-6. All those hands do is chew up your money.

YOUR HAND: A-J-A-10

A-A with any two face cards double-suited or with just one suit is a big, big hand in all forms of Omaha. In Omaha high-low the low might not come, and you have all sorts of nut-straight and nut-flush possibilities, plus you have the pair of aces. If the flop comes with all low cards, you can get away from it since it has only cost you a bet and a raise.

YOUR HAND: A-A-5-6

The only way you're thinking about playing this hand in Omaha high-low is playing the aces or the two nut-flush draws for high because the 5-6 is a tough low. But in the broad sense of the game, sometimes the A-5 or the A-6 will work for low, usually when you're heads-up and your opponent also happens to be playing high. But you'll see the flop with A-A-5-6 whether it's suited or not.

In other words, you don't enter the hand thinking that the 5-6 is going to play for a low hand. You're thinking of making the high flush or three aces—or possibly catching a 3-4, which would be a fabulous flop to this hand, giving you the straight draw and the nut-low draw. Suppose the flop comes with two little cards:

FLOP

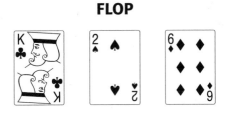

Here you have flopped a draw to the second nut low and an overpair. Against this flop, I'm through with the hand. I've seen some players take a card off, mainly because of the overpair, but also because the K♣ and 2♠ give them two backdoor flush possibilities on the flop. But I don't give as much credit to backdoor flushes as some people do. To me, that backdoor possibility is not a factor in how I play the hand; it's just an added element that might come into play. My play of a hand is based on its merit at the time.

Now suppose the flop comes:

FLOP

I'm going to play this hand on the flop. There is always the chance that the deuce or trey has counterfeited somebody else's hand for low, as opposed to the K-2-6 flop, which probably wouldn't completely counterfeit anybody's low. Suppose you draw and out pops the A♦ on the turn:

TURN

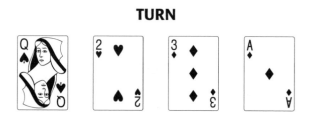

There's a strong possibility that someone has the 4-5 and has made a wheel, so what do you do now? You never lead at the pot, you trail with it. That's all you can do. But if there is a bet and raise before the action gets to you, you're throwing this hand away. Somebody already has the wheel so what are you doing here? Drawing to catch a 4 to tie for the low, or hoping to pair the board to win one-half of the pot?

Now let's say that the flop comes:

FLOP

You have the second-nut low draw and the nut flush draw. You play the hand on the flop, of course. Again the A♦ comes on the turn:

TURN

There's a strong possibility that someone has the 4-5 and has made a wheel, so what do you do now? You never lead at the pot, you trail with it. That's all you can do. But if there is a

Now how do you play the hand?

You go for it. In this scenario, you have a playing hand with a lot of outs.

YOUR HAND: A-10-9-6

I would just throw this hand away in Omaha split, because there is no low draw. Our rule in Omaha high-low is to play hands that have scoop potential, but the only way you can scoop with this hand is on the high end. You could play it around back—on the button or one spot in front of it—in an unraised pot if you don't think it'll get raised. But I wouldn't play it in a raised pot. You definitely would not play the A-6 for a low hand. As far as I'm concerned, the A-4 is the worst low hand I want to draw to for low.

YOUR HAND: 3-4-5-5

I would never voluntarily play this hand in the split game because it's a trap hand. If the flop comes A-6-small or if comes with an ace and one small overcard to your hand, you can really get trapped looking for a deuce. So, the best thing to do is not even play it to begin with. An ace-deuce on the flop is what you're looking for—and it happens sometimes—but that's too much to hope for.

I call this a trap hand because it seems that you invariably flop something to it and get caught up in the action. For example, what happens if you catch a 5 on the flop? Suppose the flop comes K-J-5.

FLOP

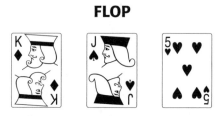

You have third set, which is always dangerous in any style of Omaha. If the board pairs, you're just hoping the other guy doesn't have a pair of kings or jacks. And if it doesn't pair, you sure don't want to see another high straight card on the turn. Your only out may be another 5 or runner-runner A-2 or 2-6 for a low straight in the split game—or even in pot-limit and limit Omaha high.

Suppose you're in the big blind with 3-4-5-5 and the flop comes 5-5-6, which means that there's a possibility of someone making a low on the turn or river.

YOU

FLOP

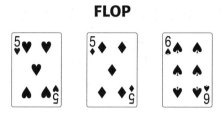

You're definitely going to lead with the hand, because you have to get whatever you can out of it. Sometimes in Omaha high-low, you'll see a player check a small full house on the flop when a low pair and another low card flop. There's no reason to give a free card in this situation because if you bet, they're going to call anyway. So why not make them pay? You always want to maximize every hand you play.

YOUR HAND: A-3-4-5

Obviously, this is a pretty good eight-or-better hand. You have the second-nut low and the rundown cards, and you can't be counterfeited. A lot of times, an ace-trey will be the best low, especially at the higher limits. Your key cards are a deuce and a 6, and ideally, you'd like to see both of them come on the flop. Even better, you'd like to see two cards in your suit along with them.

YOUR HAND: 5-6-6-7

Don't play this hand in Omaha split, period. This is strictly a losing hand.

YOUR HAND: 10-9-8-7

You would not consider playing this hand in the split game unless you're in the big or little blind in an unraised pot and you're stiffed in—period. Again, don't play the middle cards in this game. You have no way of scooping the pot unless the flop comes absolutely perfect for high and no low gets there.

YOUR HAND: Q-J-10-9

I don't like this hand in eight-or-better. I might take a flop to it hoping for high cards, but if the flop comes with low cards I dump it. This isn't a hand that I would want to play from an early position, but I might play it from around back, particularly in a multiway pot.

If I'm in the middle with three people already in the pot, I might call, figuring that most of them have come in with low cards. Once again, I have to size up my opponents and decide who is playing what. In the split game, it's very easy to size up the players because so many hands are shown down, but it's amazing how many people are staring into space or talking to somebody, not paying attention, when hands are turned over at the end.

YOUR HAND: Q-J-10-10

Obviously you take a flop to this hand in the split game. If the flop comes with little cards, you release the hand. And if it comes with big cards that give you a wrap, a set, or a made straight, and it looks like you could scoop the pot, you play it strong. That's pretty cut and dried. Whenever you have a high hand in eight-or-better and the flop comes high, you play the hand the same way that you would play it in limit Omaha high.

If even one low card comes on the flop, some weak players with premium low cards will take a card off to try to catch runner-runner low cards—just one more reason for you to play strong when you catch a two-card high flop with this type of hand. Remember that more scooped pots are won by high hands when the board comes high than they are with nut-nut hands, the wheel and top flush, for example.

YOUR HAND: 5-6-7-8

The only time that this hand should be played in eight-or-better is when you're in the big blind in an unraised pot and you're stiffed in. To continue past the flop would require a perfect scenario.

YOUR HAND: K-K-2-3

You probably have to take a flop with this hand in the eight-or-better game, but this is a trap hand. If an ace hits on the flop, you have a low draw and nothing else, no backup for your 2-3. You want to flop a king to it, of course, or an ace suited to two low cards in either clubs or hearts, giving you the nut-flush and the nut low on the flop. But don't count on it!

I'd probably call a bet with this hand before the flop, but I don't want to stand any raises with it. If an ace hits the board, your kings are nullified, and then you're just playing for low. Actually, there are so many traps in this hand that I recommend you don't play it at all.

YOUR HAND: K-Q-2-3

Now let's take a look at a trap hand that I see being played in Omaha high-low, especially at the lower limits:

I've seen a lot of players come in with this type of hand, the K-Q-2-3 single- or double-suited, particularly from around back in the low-limit split games. It might look playable, but the hand has no nut-flush cards and no backup to the 2-3. In fact, I can't think of any Omaha game in which I would play this hand, either single- or double-suited.

YOUR HAND: Q-Q-J-9

I don't play this hand in eight-or-better. You have no chance at all for the low end and the pair of queens isn't one of the top two pair.

YOUR HAND: Q-J-10-8

This is not a hand that I recommend playing in the split game unless you're in late position in a multiway pot or are stiffed in with it in one of the blinds. As long as your high cards can connect with an ace, you're in jockeying position to win either the high end or possibly scoop the whole pot if an ace comes on the board and a third low card doesn't come. You want the ace on the board because without it you're probably not going to get any action. You'll see some players come in with this hand from up front, especially guys who usually play limit hold'em, but it's a trap hand. I don't like it in Omaha high-low because it's just too much trouble to bother with.

YOUR HAND: 2-3-4-5

You can play this hand in the split game in an unraised pot, but unless you catch the ace on the flop, this can really be a really bad trap hand. Let's say the flop comes 8-6-3. You have the low straight draw and a pair—and that's fine—but you only have the 2-4 for low. When the money starts going it, somebody's going to have A-2 and you'll be trailing all the way. Boy, that can be dangerous.

If there has been a lot of action before the flop, you pretty much know that at least two or three, and maybe all of the aces are out, which decreases your chances of catching an ace on the flop. Some players like to play this hand in the right spot, and they also like to play any four wheel cards, which isn't always such a bad idea. Just remember that if you count the number of times that you flop to these types of hands versus the number of times that you don't, it doesn't measure up. That's why you always like to have an A-2 or A-3 in your low-draw hand, so that if the flop comes with low cards, you have a good shot at it.

YOUR HAND: A-J-9-7

I wouldn't play this hand at all in the eight-or-better game because I just don't see any value in it—certainly not enough to invest any money in it.

YOUR HAND: K-J-9-8

I don't play this hand at all in Omaha high-low, not even in tournaments. You have a jack-high flush possibility and could make some high straights, but you can get in a lot of trouble with this hand. It just isn't worth it.

YOUR HAND: A-K-5-6

This is a hand that may have some value at a shorthanded table. You have two cards that work with big cards, and you have three cards that work with small cards. A lot of times when you're playing shorthanded (four or fewer players), you aren't up against the nuts for the low. And you wouldn't worry as much about drawing to a king-high flush in a shorthanded game as you would in a full ring game.

OPTIMUM FLOPS

FLOP A   FLOP B

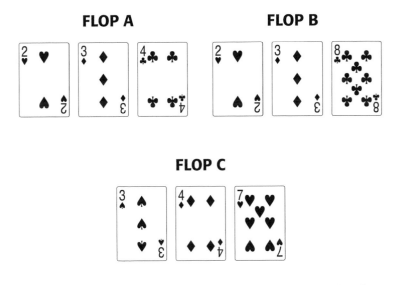

FLOP C

The optimum flop is 2-3-4, but 2-3-8 and similar flops should be also fine. A 3-4-7 would give you the nut straight and second-nut low on the flop. As I say, playing this hand shorthanded is acceptable, but the chances are high that you will get trapped with it in a full ring. You might also play the hand toward the late stages of a tournament—again, in a shorthanded situation.

POT LIMIT & LIMIT
HIGH HANDS
IN ACTION

POT-LIMIT & LIMIT HIGH HANDS IN ACTION

T.J. Cloutier

YOUR HAND: A-A-2-3

Pot-Limit Omaha

You slow down with this hand in pot-limit. I would only play it strong if I could reraise with the aces where the raise is coming in to me, hoping to isolate with one or two other players. Remember that you can reraise with aces, but you don't raise with them.

You're in danger with this hand if the flop comes something like 4-5-9 and none of your suit. If someone else has the 8-7-6-5 and is drawing to a higher straight, you're in trouble because the best straight you can make is a 6-high. Although this is the best starting hand in high-low, you have to be careful with it in pot-limit.

Interestingly, you can be aggressive in the high-low game with the best pot-limit starting hand—the A-J-A-10 double-suited—but you cannot be aggressive in pot-limit with the best high-low starting hand. If you have A-J-A-10 in high-low and no low comes on the flop, you have the opportunity to scoop the pot. But with A-A-2-3 in pot-limit, the number of good hands that will hold up are far fewer, so you play it softer than you would in the high-low game.

Limit Omaha High

In limit Omaha high, I definitely would put in one preflop raise with the two aces if they are single-suited or double-suited. It's always nice to have at least one suit, and you're in hog heaven when you have two. But if the aces are unsuited, I would not raise before the flop.

YOUR HAND: A-2-3-4

Pot-Limit Omaha and Limit Omaha High

This is not a playable hand in the high games unless you happen to get stiffed in with it and catch the absolute optimum flop to it. Otherwise, do not play it. Sure, you have a suited ace, but other than that, this is a nothing hand.

YOUR HAND: K-K-Q-J

Obviously, the K-K-Q-J double-suited is a powerful hand—as long as an ace doesn't hit the board. If an ace flops and you haven't hit any of your cards, your hand is only second best and you'll need to release it.

Suppose the flops comes:

FLOP

That ace makes you second best, so you'll need to dump that hand as quickly as you can, despite the straight draw with the 10. Your K-K-Q-J started strong, but that's how it goes in Omaha. The flop changes everything.

Notice that the board has come with three suits and two of them are yours, one heart and one club. Even though the ace is out there, when one card in each of their suits is also on the board, a lot of people say to themselves "I have two backdoor flushes," and they play the hand anyway. This is not a good move. As I said earlier, fourth street can kill you because it almost always seems to give you another flush card. If that happens, you've picked up the flush draw on the turn, and you're thinking, "Well, I can make the big flush at the river and win this pot."

Almost invariably, you aren't going to make it. When you're hoping for runner-runner, the odds against you are just too high to go for it. I don't care if you have two three-flushes, it isn't worth playing.

Now suppose the board comes 2-7-10.

FLOP

You check it, hoping that you'll get a showdown pot or that you'll pick up a king or something on fourth street. I wouldn't get involved with the hand just because I have a big overpair. If somebody bets, I'd get rid of it. If you haven't raised with this hand going in, what's the point? You don't have that much invested.

This is a raising hand in pot-limit Omaha, but if you get reraised you have a piece of cheese. In limit Omaha high, you play the hand more, that is, you might play that top pair. But in pot-limit Omaha, if an ace hits the board or if there's any action on the flop, two kings is nothing.

Now suppose the flop comes 8-8-6.

FLOP

If you put a guy on a stone bluff in the high games and you're trying to pick him off, you can consider making a play. But this is where intuition and watching the play comes in. You need to know who will try to run a bluff and who won't. Most of the time you'd better go south for the winter when you have K-K-Q-J and the board shows a low pair like 8-8-6. That's all there is to it.

Omaha is a game of peddling the nuts. Players do it a lot more in the Omaha games than they ever do in hold'em. If you're sitting there with a king-high flush and a guy is leading at you putting money in the pot, your king-high flush suddenly is like a 3-high flush—and I've never seen one of those! He has the ace-high flush 90 percent of the time. Once in a while, somebody might play that lone ace bluff at a flush when he has the ace of the suit, but not very often.

If the flop comes with three clubs, there are some players who think they have a real hand with a 10-high flush. They think they have the stone nuts and you can't get them out of the pot for all the tea in China. Naturally, you want to play against these kinds of guys, but real players are going to show you a hand. When the money gets there, real players are there.

There are situations that arise in every poker game in which you have to go away from what you should do and play what you know. Sometimes, you have to play the player, just like you do in hold'em. Who's playing the hand against you? How do they play? Are they good players? Are they weak players? But always remember that anybody, weak or strong, can be dealt a good hand. The real skill comes down to whether your instincts are right or wrong in these types of situations.

YOUR HAND: 9-9-8-7

Pot-Limit Omaha and Limit Omaha High

In limit Omaha high, I'll play the 9-9-8-7, but I don't want to stand a raise with it. I just come in for the original bet, and if I get raised, I'll release it unless there is three- or four-way action. In that case, I'm getting good enough odds to play this hand. If I pot one guy on aces and another on kings—ideally I'd like to have a good enough read to put them both on aces—then I'm playing live cards, which is what I need to bust those guys.

Now suppose the flop comes:

FLOP

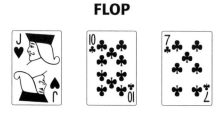

Here's a flop where you have made a straight but don't have any opportunity to improve. If there's more than one player giving action in this hand, you're supposed to throw it away. This flop cancels out any idea you might have had about making a set, and there's a flush draw out there. If you have to go against two other hands, you're actually a dog, even though you flopped the nuts. Remember, pot-limit Omaha is the only game in which you can flop the nuts, throw it away, and never lose any money.

In limit Omaha high, if you're raised on the flop, you're going to play the hand until something hits the board that can beat you. Then you release it. But if you flop the nuts in pot-limit Omaha and you bet then get raised in a couple of spots—or if one guy bets, another calls, you raise, and they both call—you're a dog.

Now let's suppose the flop comes 9-9-5.

FLOP

In pot-limit, you can check your quads, but in limit games, I would always lead at the pot and hope that someone plays back at me. There's nothing wrong with leading with huge hands, hoping that you get played with—especially in limit poker. In pot-limit, I would let my opponent take the lead on the flop and just flat call, so that I can punish him on fourth and fifth streets.

YOUR HAND: A-J-A-10

Pot-Limit Omaha and Limit Omaha High

A-A with any two face cards double-suited or with just one suit is a big, big hand in all forms of Omaha. As far as I'm concerned, this is the best hand you can have in pot-limit Omaha. With this hand, and this one only, I'll go away from my rule of never being the original raiser with aces before the flop. I will raise before the flop from any position, in all three types of Omaha games.

If you have A-A-J-10 the board might even come with 10-10-4, giving you top set with top kicker and overcards. Even if someone has two fours in the hole, for example, there are still cards that you can hit—the jack, the aces—that will take him off the hand. So you still have a strong hand.

In Omaha high-low the low might not come, and you have all sorts of nut-straight and nut-flush possibilities, plus you have the pair of aces. If the flop comes with all low cards, you can get away from it since it has only cost you a bet and a raise.

In pot-limit or limit Omaha, if you get any kind of connected flop to this hand, you're going with it because it's such a big hand.

Suppose the flop comes K-Q-8 with two cards in one of your suits.

FLOP

You have a monster—an overpair, a double middle-buster, and a flush draw. You have nine flush cards and six straight cards, plus the two aces. You have 17 outs with two cards to come, which means you have 34 pure wins.

You have to play those kinds of hands!

In most of the straights that you want to draw to in high Omaha, there should be three or four cards that can make it for you. If you play an open-ender in hold'em, you just have eight wins, but in Omaha you want to have more wins than that. The key in Omaha high is having a big hand and drawing at an even bigger hand so that you can cut off other players. If they make their hand, you're there too. You have to think about all these things as you're playing.

Now let's look at another flop:

FLOP

This may not look like that great a flop at first glance, but do you see what you have here? A single middle buster, an overpair and a flush draw—a lot of ways to make the hand.

Now let's take a look at what might happen in Omaha when the board pairs and you have an overpair. Suppose the 8 pairs on the turn:

TURN

Against any action, you have to give it up. But what if there is no action? If someone checks to you, you also check. Sometimes you can win in high Omaha with aces-up when the board pairs like this, but why would you lead at it with a bet on the end? All somebody needs to beat you is one little 8.

In pot-limit it's not just wasting a bet, it's more than that. It's like betting a four-flush with one card to come—you make the bet, somebody comes over the top of you, and then you have to dump the hand. When the board pairs, all you have with those aces-up is a draw with one card to come. There's a big difference. Once that board pairs, it's check-down time.

If somebody leads at it big, you act according to who the player is and what you've seen him do on the end. Suppose he checks after the board pairs the 8, then a blank comes on the river, and he leads at it. Now you're put to the decision. What you decide to do depends on what you know about this player. How good a player is he? Would he bluff at this pot? Could he have two jacks in the hole, or maybe a lone queen? What could you beat with aces up?

Remember, don't try to invent a hand that you can beat. Don't call unless you think you can win the pot with the hand you have.

YOUR HAND: A-A-5-6

Pot-Limit Omaha and Limit Omaha High

A-A-5-6 double-suited is a good hand in pot-limit and limit Omaha high. But without a suit in pot-limit, this is a reraising hand only if you think that you can isolate the field to one other player. You don't want to go against three or four players without being double suited.

In both pot-limit Omaha and limit Omaha high, you're looking for nut flushes or three aces with this hand. A 2-3-4 flop would be fabulous, and a 3-4-7 would be great because you would have the nuts. Even if an 8 hit the board on the turn, you would still have the nuts.

GOOD FLOPS TO A-A-5-6 DOUBLE SUITED

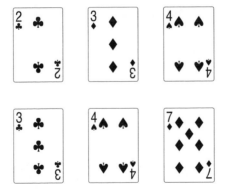

BAD FLOP TO A-A-5-6 DOUBLE SUITED

In the long run, this is a good hand when you get certain flops to it, but you don't want to see a middle flop. For example, if an 8-7-2 came on the flop, you're a goner. In this scenario, the optimum card to catch is a 4 but if a 9, 10, or jack hits the board, somebody could have an upstairs wrap and you could be a gone goose. Naturally, you're never looking to make the bottom end of a straight, especially in a multiway pot.

You're looking to make a big flush with this hand and just hoping the board doesn't pair after you make it. Any time the board pairs in pot-limit Omaha, be very, very careful. It's like a red light suddenly flashing. When the board pairs in Omaha high-low, it's less serious because if three low cards are out there and you have the nut low, you can still win part of the pot. And high-low is a limit game, so you can't get killed in it. The same goes for limit Omaha high. But in pot-limit Omaha, you can get flat busted.

In a big pot-limit ring game, I saw two hands played that illustrate this point. The flop comes Q-8-2, giving David "Devilfish" Ulliott three queens, and Sammy Farquhar is in the pot with him. Devilfish leads at it and Sammy calls. On fourth street comes a 5. Devilfish bets at it, Sammy raises, and Devilfish calls him.

Sammy doesn't see that David has a $5,000 chip, so he just raises for the blacks that he sees in front of him. At the river comes a 9. Sammy bets $3,400, the amount Ulliott has left.

Devilfish says, "You got a J-10 in your hand?"

And I'm thinking, "Looks to me like Sammy has a queen and was trying to double-pair to win the pot, playing in a short three-handed game, then ended up making the other straight that was possible, the 9-8-7-6-5." And that's exactly what happened: Sammy caught runner-runner and backdoored the straight to win the pot against the three queens.

Devilfish went crazy. He said that the only thing he was hoping was that a 9, 10, or jack didn't come on the end, because if Sammy had had a Q-J-10-9, then he would have had a legitimate hand to play, you see. But the way some of those guys play at the big limits, they don't have a legitimate hand a lot of times.

This just shows how Murphy's Law works in Omaha: Anything that can go wrong, will go wrong. And things like this will happen even more often in limit Omaha high because players don't have to call as much money to draw. For that reason, more pots are played multiway in limit than in pot-limit.

In limit Omaha high, this is a very good hand, a raising hand when it's double- or single-suited. But without a suit, I don't think this is a raising hand in any variety of Omaha.

YOUR HAND: A-10-9-6

Pot-Limit Omaha

This isn't much of a hand, but it is a playing hand if it's suited, and you can play it in an unraised pot. Obviously, what you're looking for is K-Q-J, three cards in your suit, or something like 8-7-5, which would be a helluva flop.

If I had this hand, a Q-J-8 would be another wraparound I'd like, but I don't want to see just a Q-J-x with no suits out there, because then all I'd have is an open-end straight, and in Omaha I don't want just an open-end straight draw.

Other than a flop that gives you three of one of your cards, a flush, the 8-7-5, or the Q-J-8, the optimum drawing flop is one that has either a Q-J or an 8-7 in it, plus two cards in your suit. That way, you have wraps. Even an 8-7-4 flop would be okay, especially if it also has two of your suit in it.

Limit Omaha High

I would always take a flop to this hand in limit Omaha high, even in a raised pot, because it won't cost me as much to see the flop as it might in pot-limit. If you get involved with this hand in pot-limit—if you come in early with it and then get raised—what do you do? If you call the raise and don't flop to it, you've invested a lot of money. But in limit games, you've only invested one more unit, and you can get away from it cheaply if you don't flop to the hand.

YOUR HAND: 3-4-5-5

Pot-Limit Omaha

The only way that this hand would come up for me in pot-limit Omaha is if I'm in the blind or if I decide to call a single bet, hoping to take off an opponent who I'm sure is playing a big pair. If you can isolate some of the big pairs, sometimes you can take a flop and win a big, big pot. This is one of the finer points of playing pot-limit. But generally speaking, this is not a hand that I recommend playing.

Limit Omaha High

You might take a flop to this hand in the limit game. If you don't hit the flop, you simply get rid of it.

YOUR HAND: A-3-4-5

Pot-Limit Omaha and Limit Omaha High

You can call the original bet with this hand, but you shouldn't call a raise with it. If the flop comes with little cards that connect, you're in pretty good shape.

When you play a hand like this, you're looking for a flop with a 2 and/or a 6 in it, because those are your key cards. Suppose the flop comes 2-4-5. Although you have the wheel, you could already be up against a 6-high straight and drawing for your life trying to catch a 6 to tie for the high end of the pot—unless the 6 makes an 8-high straight for somebody else!

YOUR HAND: 5-6-6-7

Pot-Limit Omaha

In pot-limit this is a takeoff hand, a hand similar to the 3-4-5-5 that might allow you to beat those guys with the big pairs if a 6 or a low wrap comes on the flop. You can play it from around back, however, you don't want to stand a raise with it, especially if you're heads-up, because you know that your opponent is liable to have aces, kings, or a big wrap up-top double-suited.

The reason we're showing this hand double-suited is to demonstrate how having the low flush draw can really get you in trouble sometimes. You could make a 7-high flush in clubs or a 6-high flush in hearts and be deader than a doornail. Actually, you don't want to have a flush draw with this hand; if that's all you have, get rid of it. But if you flop a straight or a set—a reason to stay in the hand—a backdoor flush could come in for you. If that happens, you won't necessarily need to have a big flush because backdoor flushes can be weaker and still win the pot. But the point is that you're never betting a flush draw as the optimum part of the hand.

In pot-limit Omaha, the main strength of this hand and hands similar to it is their takeoff value against people who are playing big pairs. Suppose there's a little raise followed by three or four callers. In this case, there's nothing wrong with calling the raise because you know they are most likely playing big cards, and your little cards are probably live. After all, there are 52 cards in that deck, and you have a chance to take them off their big hands if you can catch the little cards.

Limit Omaha High

You can take a flop with this hand and hope to catch something to it, such as a wraparound, a full house, anything you can get. A straight flush? Dreamer!

YOUR HAND: 10-9-8-7

Pot-Limit Omaha

This is just the normal type of decent rundown hand that you're trying to get a flop to in pot-limit. The general rule is that if there are three players in the pot in addition to you, you might stand a raise with this hand, hoping that you flop a wrap.

You could flop a lot of different cards that would give you nut draws. Suppose the flop comes with a 6-5, 7-6, 8-6, or 9-6.

These are all bottom-end straight cards that you want to see. You don't want the top-end cards out there. If a Q-J comes down, you could be dead already, so you're always thinking of catching the bottom end to this hand.

Obviously, the best flop you could get is 6-5-4 in three suits, but catching it is very unlikely.

Limit Omaha High

You play this hand about the same way you would in pot-limit. You can stand a raise with it suited or unsuited. If you don't flop to it, get rid of it. Suppose the flop comes with a J-7-4, giving you an inside wrap to the J-7. But then suppose a queen comes off on the turn.

TURN

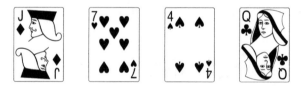

Now you really don't know where you are in the hand. If somebody has a wrap to the king, you're really in trouble. Get the drift?

You have to be very careful with this hand. You want to flop the low end of the straight because if a higher card comes off that promotes the strength of your hand, then you'll also have the chance of making an even higher straight. Remember that you always want to be able to draw to a bigger hand than the one you have already made.

In the limit game you can play this type of hand more strongly than you would in the pot-limit game, and you also would play it longer. In pot-limit you might have to lay it down if the flop comes with two cards in a suit that isn't yours;

otherwise it would be pretty hard to lay it down if two of your key cards come on the flop. Remember that in the limit game there are more cards that you can play deeper into the hand.

Other obviously strong flops to this hand include 10-10-9, 9-9-8, 9-9-7, and 10-10-10 would really be nice!

STRONG FLOP A   ### STRONG FLOP B

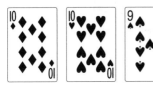
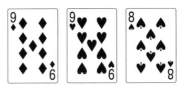

STRONG FLOP C   ### STRONG FLOP D

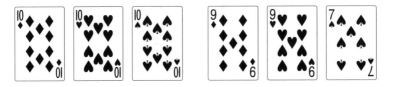

YOUR HAND: Q-J-10-9

Pot-Limit Omaha and Limit Omaha High

I like this hand. If you get this hand in limit Omaha high, you're getting to the point where suits could come into play.

However, if you make a flush, you'll have to be very leery of it. You wouldn't want to lead with the flush; you would have to play it soft.

This is another good rundown hand, and if you flop a wrap, you'll be drawing at the nuts at all times. You could also flop the nuts or two pair to the hand. If the flop comes Q-J-2, for example, and there isn't much action, you probably have the best hand. Somebody may have the big wrap to it, but even with two pair, you still have the bottom wrap. And if the turn comes with an 8, you'll have the nuts.

YOUR HAND: Q-J-10-10

Pot-Limit Omaha and Limit Omaha High

This is a playing hand. If you catch a 10 on the flop and that's the top card on the board, you're in great shape. If the flop comes with a K-9 or an A-K you have the inside wrap. If it comes 9-8-7, that's terrific because you have the best hand with a draw to a higher hand.

The best possible flop would be 10-9-8, top set and a made straight. If it comes two of the same suit, you would play it soft. But wait—if it comes 10-9-8 with two suited cards, I don't see how you could play it soft! You can't because you still have top set and a made straight. You might get raised by the big flush draw, but you sure as hell have to play it to see one more card at least.

YOU

PLAY THIS FLOP SOFT

DON'T PLAY THIS FLOP SOFT

If the flush draw makes the nuts on the turn, he's coming after you. Then, of course, you are no longer the favorite, but stuff happens, you know? On the other hand, if there are only two flush cards on the turn, then you're a huge favorite.

Now suppose you catch this flop:

FLOP

You're in a four-way pot, and there has been action before the flop. You've flopped middle set and don't know where you are in the hand. This is a good example of when it comes down to playing the players.

You look around and ask, "Who raises with aces before the flop? Who doesn't?" You know the answers because you have watched how your opponents have been playing.

Suppose you lead off with second set and a player who never raises with aces before the flop raises you. You know that he doesn't raise coming in with aces in order not to tip his hand off. Now you're put to the decision as to whether or not he has three aces. Most of the time he would have them, especially with a broken board.

You figure that your top players will not raise with the inside wrap on this type of flop, especially not with the ace looking them in the face. They might raise with a big wrap before the flop, but not on the flop, because the ace is out there. So, what is your opponent raising with? This is where your playing skill comes in. These are the decisions for which you can't write down any cut and dried advice. Your decision depends on the situation, and you have to make up your mind about how to play it.

If you're playing the limit high game and there was action before the flop, a lot of your straight cards may already be out. In a multiway pot, for example, the cards you need to make your high straight might not be available to you because they're already in other players' hands. You have to take this point into consideration.

For example, say that you play K-K-Q-J in a raised pot in a limit Omaha high game, and all your opponents come in. The flop comes A-10-7. Now you have to make up your mind as to whether any of your cards are still in the deck. In this hand with this flop, the pair of kings isn't even entering into the mix. It's the middle wrap that you're looking at.

YOUR HAND: 5-6-7-8

Pot-Limit Omaha

You can play this middle rundown hand in pot-limit, but you don't want to stand a raise with it. If you can come in cheaply, why not try it? If you catch a flop to it, you're in hog heaven but if you don't, you dump it. Just remember that if you flop a straight to it with two of the same suit on the board and you get any action, don't be afraid to throw it away. Overall, this isn't a hand that I would feel very enthusiastic about.

Limit Omaha High

You can call a bet or a single raise with this hand in the high Omaha game. I might even come in with it from up-front, but if I don't catch a big flop to it, I would throw it away. Suited or unsuited, the hand plays the same.

You're not looking to make a flush since you don't have a nut-flush draw and almost any opponent could have a flush draw higher than yours, unless you flop a straight flush, of course. If you flop a straight to it, you would take off a card on fourth street, even if the board is double-suited. After all, you have the nuts.

Naturally, you don't want to flop a J-10-9; you want a baby flop. A flop like 10-9-5 is an okay flop, but remember that you can't get any bigger while somebody who's playing K-Q-J-10 has the top-end straight draw. The bottom line is that this is a playable hand in the limit game but you have to be careful with it.

YOUR HAND: K-K-2-3

Pot-Limit Omaha

You have to take a flop to this hand but you do not raise with it, and you don't want to stand a raise with it. You want to catch a king or an ace suited to one of your suits. But be very careful with this hand, especially in pot-limit. It's another one of those hands that could cost you a lot of money. With this hand, you can get broke, and that's no joke.

Limit Omaha High

In the limit game you'll see a flop with the hand and then play it pretty much the same way you would in pot-limit.

YOUR HAND: K-Q-2-3

The K-Q-2-3 single- or double-suited might look playable, but I can't think of any Omaha game in which I would play this hand, either single- or double-suited. It is a huge trap hand and you shouldn't play it.

YOUR HAND: Q-Q-J-9

Pot-Limit Omaha and Limit Omaha High

You'll see the flop in both the pot-limit and limit high games with this hand. In pot-limit you have a lot of possibilities with the hand. Flushes aren't something you're looking for, but if it comes runner-runner on the turn and river and the nut flush isn't out there, a flush could win the pot.

Obviously, you want to flop a queen or rundown cards. You especially want to flop a 10, your key card, with at least one other straight card. Flopping a split board like Q-7-2 would be pretty nice, too!

YOUR HAND: Q-J-10-8

Pot-Limit Omaha and Limit Omaha High

With only one gap, this is definitely a playable hand in the high games, but I don't want to stand too much pressure with it. This is a pretty nice rundown hand but I need to hit perfect, and I don't like any hand that I have to hit perfect.

An A-K is a good flop because nobody can make a higher straight, and a K-9 is ideal. If you flop a Q-J, you might not like it too much because even though you have top two pair, there probably would be all sorts of straight draws out against you. It's a hand that you have to be very careful with. You hope to flop the nuts and that no suits come out. This is just a medium quality hand way down in the rankings.

YOUR HAND: 2-3-4-5

Pot-Limit Omaha and Limit Omaha High

I won't play this hand in the two high Omaha games. It's just too low a rundown hand.

YOUR HAND: A-J-9-7

Pot-Limit Omaha and Limit Omaha High

This hand gives you a lot of opportunities to make the nuts in the high games. Look at it closely: You could catch a K-Q-10, a 10-8-6, or a 10-8 for a wraparound draw. You wouldn't necessarily want to catch a Q-10-8, even though you'd have the nut straight at the moment, because if you're up against a straight draw with a king in it, you could get outdrawn.

If two clubs come on the flop, you'll have the nut-flush draw. If a spade comes on the flop as well, you'll have a backdoor flush possibility with your J-7 suited. If the flop comes with two spades and nothing else that fit my hand, I would never play the J-7 for a flush draw, although I might call a bet.

The best feature of this hand is that you can flop a lot of straights to it that are nut straights. In a ring game, I would play it from up front. Of course, I'd have to decide in advance how much pressure I would be willing to take with it, but this is definitely a playable hand.

YOUR HAND: K-J-9-8

Pot-Limit Omaha and Limit Omaha High

In pot-limit and limit Omaha high where you only play high hands, a K-J-9-8 might be a playable hand. Obviously, if you don't flop to it, you can get away from the hand. I don't really consider the J-8 flush draw to be an important element in the hand, but if the flop comes with cards such as 10-7-x or Q-10-x, you'll have a big wrap.

FLOPS WITH BIG WRAPS

FLOP A   FLOP B

FLOPS WITH UPSTAIRS WRAPS

FLOP A   FLOP B

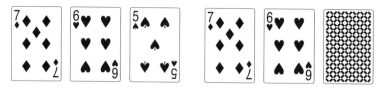

If it comes with a 7-6-5 or 7-6-x, you'll have the upstairs wrap. So it isn't really too bad a hand in either pot-limit or limit high, although I wouldn't want to have to stand a raise with it in pot-limit.

In limit Omaha high, I might play this hand from any position. If I had limped in from a front or middle position, I would call a raise. But in pot-limit, you have to be more careful about your position when you play this type of hand, because if you get raised, you can get involved for a lot of money. If that happens, you would have to flop the stone joint to the hand to continue further.

YOUR HAND: A-K-5-6

Pot-Limit Omaha and Limit Omaha High

I don't give this hand any credence whatsoever in pot-limit. I just couldn't force myself to play it; I couldn't stand any action with it. If I get raised before the flop, what am I looking for? A 2-3-4, 3-4-7, three cards of the same rank as any one of my cards, or two cards of the same rank as one of mine and one card of the same rank as one of my other cards—and that's about it.

GOOD FLOPS

FLOP A   FLOP B

FLOP C   FLOP D

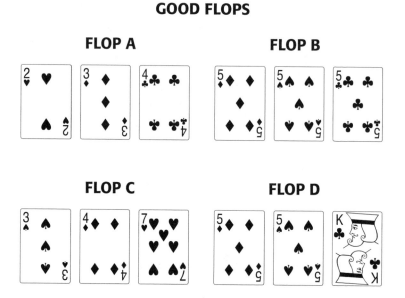

It has a little more value in limit than it does in pot-limit, but I'm going to let somebody else play this one!

THE TOURNAMENT TRAIL: TACTICS & TALES

THE TOURNAMENT TRAIL: TACTICS AND TALES

T.J. Cloutier

If everybody played alike, poker would just be a hand holding contest, and the best hand would always win. Over a period of time, the cards would break even and nobody would be a winner. Everybody would be even. But that's not the way it works. Some people play better than others.

POKER IS A GAME OF MISTAKES

Poker is a game of mistakes. No poker player plays perfectly on every hand, but if you let your opponents make the majority of mistakes, you're going to win the money.

For example, in a recent no-limit hold'em tournament, the first man brought it in for a raise and the second man reraised. I'm sitting right next to him, and I have two aces. I move in. The first man throws his hand away and the second man calls with two queens when he has no chance—*no* chance. We were down to twelve players in the tournament, and there was no way in the world that his two queens could be good after I had put in the third raise. But he called and doubled me up.

This is a perfect example of the mistakes players make. You have to use your head in these situations. Anybody worth his salt knows better than to make that call. The fewer mistakes you make, the better you'll come out at the end of the day, the month, the year. Over a year's time, mistakes are the dividing line between profit and loss. In the short run, of course, luck comes into the equation.

Remember this: A mistake that you make in a ring game where you can go to your pocket for more money will be magnified ten times in a tournament. It is ten times worse to commit that same mistake in a tournament as it is to make it in a cash game.

LOW-LIMIT REBUY TOURNAMENTS

People have asked me if they should take more chances in the small rebuy tournaments. I've seen some people playing real loose in those events, trying to get a hold of a lot of chips early, but I think that's wrong. I'll tell you why: You can't win in the first hour or two and that's all there is to it. Nobody's ever won the tournament in the first three hours either, and that's the amount of time many of these tournaments allow for rebuys.

When you enter a tournament, you're putting up a certain amount, hoping to win a particular percentage over that. Every time you rebuy, you knock your percentage down a notch. I'm not saying you shouldn't rebuy, but if you should, only do it if you've had something legitimate beat and you lost your original buy-in, not because you gave it away. And make sure it was a real hand that got beat, because if you had $500 to start with, and you've lost it, all you'll get in the rebuy is the $500 that you started with. It's not as though you're increasing your stack—you're right back on square one.

I'm all in favor of the add-on to increase your chips, but make sure you've had something beat before you make a rebuy. Try to play on that first buy-in; play it like you were playing a no-rebuy tournament. Why should you rebuy? Let the other players do that—they'll build the pot for you.

In some tournaments you can't rebuy until you run out of chips or fall below a certain amount. In others you can rebuy right away. If you're playing a limit tournament that has one optional rebuy and one add-on, and if you're planning on sacrificing, say, $1,500 to the tournament, then I suggest rebuying right away and then taking the add-on. But I would never do it in pot-limit Omaha because of the beats you can take for your whole stack. You might need the rebuy for your comeback stake.

OMAHA HIGH-LOW STRATEGY

Here is an important point that Tom and I stress in all our books: In tournaments you can't go back into your pocket. So when you play a hand, you'd better damn well like the hand. And you'd better play it in a good situation, because otherwise it could cost you a lot of chips—chips that are very hard to recover.

This is why I usually won't play a hand like 2-3-4-5 in Omaha high-low tournaments. I'll play it heads-up or three-handed, but in a full ring game I won't play it. I don't want to get stiffed and get loser on a hand that I know I shouldn't have been in there with in the first place.

Some players in the low buy-in tournaments come in with one high card with three wheel cards, such as K-2-3-4. You can play some of these hands in some ring games, because you've seen what the other players are playing and know that you can loosen up your action a little bit. But as far as the rules go, the K-2-3-4 isn't a hand that you should play, and neither is the

2-3-4-5. But I've played them, you've played them, we've all played them.

STARTING HANDS: NOT RECOMMENDED

Say that you're playing in a tournament and you start with $500. You're playing at the $30/$60 limit, so this hand could end up taking half of your chips very easily. You have to ask yourself, "Do I want to risk half my chips on this piece of cheese?" And you don't do it. That's the way to play.

I try to have more money at each level of the tournament. I don't care how much the increase is, I know that if I increase my stack at every level, I have a chance to win the tournament. So I let a lot of people do things that they want to do and I play my way. My way is to not get involved with hands that might eat up my chips.

Get involved when you're doing the betting—when you have the power—not when your opponents have it. If you have the patience to wait for the good hands, they will come sooner or later. In a recent no-limit tournament, I didn't hold aces or kings during the first six hours. Then, in the next two rounds, I held them once in each round.

BAD BEATS

In tournaments, you have to expect bad beats and learn to take them without going on tilt. Sometimes that's hard to do. With four tables left in the no-limit hold'em championship tournament at the Carnivale of Poker, I had $38,000 in chips. A man brought it in for a modest raise, and I called with A♥ Q♥ in the big blind. The flop came Q-3-2 in three suits. I led out with a $6,000 bet, and he moved in on me. I knew I had the best hand, so I beat him into the pot.

"You've got me," he says. "I'm bluffing." And turns over the J♠ 9♠. An 8 came on the turn and a 10 came at the river to give him a straight! If I'd won the hand, I would've had the lead in the tournament. Instead, I was out of it.

So, here's an unofficial Pro Tip: That's the way it goes— first your money, then your clothes!

PLAYING AGAINST LIMIT HOLD'EM PLAYERS

Here's another tip: A lot of limit hold'em tournament players are taking a shot at no-limit hold'em tournaments these days. The small, rebuy, no-limit tournaments are popular events in a lot of cardrooms because they give people a chance to practice big-bet poker skills. Remember that limit players are usually one-bet players. They tend to put their chips all-in a lot of the time.

If you're an experienced no-limit or pot-limit player, you have to take this into account, because these players have the same tendency to push in all their chips in pot-limit Omaha tournaments.

THE MORNING GLORIES

If a racehorse works out at 12 seconds per furlong, that's considered to be a real good workout, so if they go three furlongs in 36 seconds, that's very good. Now say a horse runs those three furlongs in 34 seconds—and that's flying. So the guys at the track will bet 'em down like hell when they see those workout stats. But he runs dead last in the afternoon. He's only good in the morning, so they call him a "morning glory."

Believe me, the same thing holds true in poker tournaments. Morning glories are players who get a lot of chips early in the tournament but who have no chance of winning it. Once again, let me stress that in tournaments you can't go to your pocket. Before you put chips in a pot, you should know that you have a pretty good chance of banking a profit. Morning glories don't understand this concept.

For these reasons, you should not worry about how many chips other people have early in the tournament. Play the way that you're supposed to play, and you'll have a chance to get there. If you don't, you probably won't.

At the end of the first hour of a major tournament in Southern California, a man had $50,000 in chips, five times the amount he'd started with. He had made every draw he could possibly make.

He did not make it to the second limit change.

He was the epitome of the morning glory. He kept playing the same way he had been playing very early, and suddenly, the percentages caught up with him and he couldn't make a hand.

This is what happens with morning glories. They get a lucky rush of cards early, or play some substandard starting hands that get there, and they don't adjust their play once they get a lot of chips. More often than not, they self-destruct.

INTUITION IN TOURNAMENTS

You often play by your intuition at the final table and do things that you wouldn't do while trying to get there, such as loosening up a little bit in spots against shorter stacks and things like that.

When they read about the hands that were shown down at the final table, a lot of people think they just look like trash. But at the final table, the blinds are so high that you have to adjust your starting hand standards based on what it's costing you for every round at the table. And since it's costing you a hell of a lot of money each round, you're forced to play a few more hands.

I don't know exactly what the blinds were when we finished the pot-limit Omaha tournament at the 1998 World Series of Poker, but you can bet that they were high enough that at any one time, you could have gotten all the money in. There was about $340,000 in chips at the final table, and yet the blinds were high enough that you had to play. At the finals of the 1998 eight-or-better event, there was $408,000 in chips on the table.

When the blinds become extremely high, some of the hands you'd consider marginal early in the tournament become acceptable to play late in the event. You just can't wait for the nuts when the blinds are burning up your chips. You have to be selective when you play these hands, of course, but you have to play them.

PLAYING SIDE ACTION DURING TOURNAMENTS

My bread and butter used to be the no-limit hold'em games, but then those games all dried up, leaving nothing around home to play. I started playing the tournament circuit and did well, so I stayed with it, but I don't consider myself to be a tournament specialist like Tom. I don't care whether I play in tournaments or ring games, but I don't think the two mix very well. I don't believe that you can give 100 percent of yourself to a tournament if you're also playing a lot of side action, and vice-versa. Although side action is what we all did for a good number of years, there are so many tournaments these days, that a lot of us don't have time to play the side games anymore.

Occasionally, you can play side games and tournaments too, but believe me when I tell you that it usually takes all of your energy to play a tournament. You have to concentrate very hard, and you're playing for a lot more money than you usually can make in a side game. So it takes all of your concentration to do well.

Then when you get into a side game where you know that you can win $4,000 or $5,000, you don't always have the total concentration that you need to win. I think that a person can focus on something for only so long before his brain has to have some time off. And that is why some tournament players don't do well in the side games. They don't play side games very often and when they do play them, they aren't giving them their full concentration.

This also is why some top tournament players have an avocation outside of poker, something else that they enjoy doing. For Tom, it's backgammon; for me, it's my marriage and golf. You need another outlet to stay balanced.

ESTABLISHING A TRACK RECORD

People have asked me what it takes to be successful on the tournament trail, suggesting things such as concentration, motivation, skill, and a big bankroll. You need those first three items in big doses, of course, but you don't necessarily need a big bankroll.

It costs a lot of money to play tournaments, that's true, but if you can establish a track record by being very successful in your tournament play, you won't have to worry about the money part. You'll get phone calls all the time from people who want a piece of your tournament action, so the money part will take care of itself. For the past fifteen years I haven't been to a single tournament where I couldn't come into town without a dime of my own and still play it if I wanted to.

But if you're not successful at tournament play—I don't care if you're the greatest player in the world in the ring games—you're going to have a hard time finding a backer. You have to have a solid track record on the tournament trail.

THE 1998 POT-LIMIT OMAHA CHAMPIONSHIP EVENT

This was a strange tournament in a way, as are many pot-limit events. A lot of people were taking rebuys early in the tournament, and there was a lot of jostling around. Players like Lindy Chambers and O'Neill Longson were in it, men who can really play the game but who like it so much that they sometimes get in real deep.

I went to the final table as the chip leader, with Doyle Brunson in second and Erik Seidel in third. The lineup also included David Mosley, a very tough player from England, and

Donnacha O'Dea, an excellent player from Ireland. Patrick Bruell, the movie star from France, played great, absolutely great, and so did Mattie Kuortti—he never got out of line. Gary Haubelt played his usual solid game as did Paul Rowe, who is also a good all-around player. So, we had a very strong, solid lineup at the final table. I took the worst of it in two or three pots, knowing that I had the worst of it. But I had such a big chip lead that I could take a few chances, trying to knock somebody out.

For most of the tournament, I basically had let the other players knock each other out, but at the final table, I took the job into my own hands. A lot of times, that's the way you have to do it when you're the one who has the big stack.

I've heard that the others might have been intimidated by Doyle and me because we were "big players with big stacks" in front of us. But I never feel intimidated by another player. I think Doyle's a fabulous player and has been for years and years, but he can't intimidate me. And I'm sure I don't intimidate him.

Erik Seidel made the big comeback in the tournament. He started off in last chip position with only $8,500 and moved up to win third place.

It was interesting that the final three at the table were Doyle, Erik, and me, since at the Four Queens no-limit hold'em event one year, the final four were Doyle Brunson, Chip Reese, Erik Seidel, and me. That was the toughest final table I've ever played in any tournament. So it was quite a coincidence that the 1998 World Series pot-limit Omaha event came down to Doyle and Erik and me.

On the end I offered to make a deal with Doyle, who was about $50,000 behind me, based on the chip count. His reply was, "If I get to where we have an even chip count, maybe we can talk then." He was at a disadvantage and didn't want to get less than half of the pot—and I don't blame him. I don't like to make deals, and I haven't offered them to very many players. I knew that there wasn't even a fraction of play between the two of us that was much different. We both could reel it in and throw it out. As it turned out, I won it for $136,000 with no deal and Doyle took second money, $78,200.

I was also at the final table of the $2,000 Omaha high-low event at the 1998 Series, where I finished fifth for $18,000 and change. Chau Giang, who is an excellent high-limit split player and the winner of the lowball title a few years back at the Series, won it, and Carl Bailey from Oklahoma took second. Brian Nadell is a top player who came in third. Of course, all of the top players are always at the World Series and other tournaments, so there's never an easy field.

TALES FROM
T.J.

TALES FROM T.J.

ALONG THE ROAD TO THE WORLD SERIES OF POKER

The thing that's missing—or is dying out fast—in the poker world these days are all the characters from the past who were such colorful guys. When people ask me about the young players coming up today, I mention that they don't have the style the old guys had. Here are stories about a few of the gamblers I used to play with in Texas and Las Vegas.

Tippy Toe Joe Shotsman

In our first book, I told the story about George McGann robbing a poker game after he got loser and nobody saying anything about it when he came back and played the next day. Now let me tell you the story about George and Joe Shotsman, who they called Tippy Toe Joe. He was an old-time poker player and a real heavy drinker back in Dallas. Tippy Toe Joe could drink more booze and still play poker than any man I've ever seen in my life. He made Bill Smith, another legendary boozer, look like a piker!

Tippy Toe would come in and start playing at 2:00 in the morning after all the bars had closed. They'd take a water glass and just fill it with whiskey, and he'd drink it like he was drinking water—and still play. He and George used to play head-up no-limit hold'em.

In this game, they'd been playing for about two weeks straight, and Tippy Toe had beat George every time they played. Tippy Toe was a much better player, but remember that George was a stone killer and always carried his gun. He was the type of guy who would meet you face to face and shoot you. If he had to shoot somebody, he'd look 'em right in the eye and then shoot 'em. Well, Tippy Toe breaks George again. So George pulls out his gun and says, "Tippy Toe, I want all the money you've got in front of you and all the money you've got in your pocket. This thing's over with and I'm getting some of my money back!"

So Tippy Toe pushes over his money and then reaches in his pocket where he has $10,000 in $100 traveler's checks. George makes Tippy Toe sign every one of those traveler's checks! Tippy Toe is pretty smart, so as he's signing these checks, he says, "Now George, this is gonna leave me awful short. Do you think you could let me keep about $3,000 so I'll have a little money on me?" Well, he talked George into loaning him back $3,000 of the money he's stealing from him!

After this is all done and they're going down the stairs from this joint, Tippy Toe looks up at George and he says, "George, we're not gonna let this little incident stand in the way of our poker game, are we?"

And that's a true story. Tippy Toe didn't want to lose George—he knew he could beat him every time they played.

A Killer of a Poker Game

McGann was a killer for hire, but he wasn't the only one who played with us. He wasn't a very big guy, he always wore a suit, and he had two guns. In the same game in Dallas there was R. D. Matthews, who used to be Benny Binion's bodyguard.

He always had a gun on him, but his big thing was hitting 'em with a baseball bat.

And there was Troy Inman, a killer who wouldn't want to face you. If he was going to kill you, he'd stand around the corner and get you as you went by. Then there was Harrelson, who killed that judge, Woods, down in San Antonio—he played in the game.

Now, they didn't all play at the same time, but they all played in that same game. They were some real characters. I'll never forget the time when I went there for the first time. I knew who Troy was, and he was running the poker game. I won about $9,000, and he paid me off. Then he says, "Now, T.J., this is a bad area so I'll walk you down the stairs and see that you get to your car."

I was more afraid of getting robbed by him than by anybody else!

Bill Smith

Bill Smith was a world champion, and he ended up playing $4/$8 hold'em at the Gold Coast poker room in his last days. But Bill Smith was one of the greatest poker players that ever lived. He was too tight when he was sober, but when he got halfway drunk, he was the best player you've ever played against. And if he got completely drunk, he just gave away his money. You could always tell when Bill was past that halfway point. If you were backing Bill Smith and you could just get him halfway drunk, you knew you were gonna win money. But he tipped you off in two different ways when he was totally drunk.

For one, he'd start totaling the flop. Say it came out there with a 10-7-4, he'd say, "21!" Then when he got up to get another drink or go to the bathroom, he'd have a little hip-hop in his step. When he did that, you knew he was gone and that was when you started playing with Bill. You knew that he was gonna bluff every pot, it didn't matter what he had. And he never slowed down—he'd just bluff, bluff, bluff.

I used to stake Bill when he was down on his luck back in Dallas. And he wouldn't bluff anybody but me! He said he could bluff me because I was staking him. Sooner or later, you get a little tired of that and you just take him off and save what money's left. He was a character.

There were these two guys: Corky Stiles and Ike White, a real nice black man who always played with us in the poker games in Dallas. Bill would get drunk in a game and lose his money and he'd say, "Give me $500, Corky." And Corky would slide him over $500. Bill would lose it in the first hand and then he'd say, "Give me $500, Ike." He'd lose it in the first hand. Then he'd go up to a thousand. He'd say, "Corky, give me $1,000." Corky would say, "Well, Bill, I'm getting a little short." And Bill would go, "I said, give me a thousand!" And they'd shove it over to him. Bill wasn't a mean guy, but he'd get belligerent when he just wanted to play.

He traveled that Southern circuit all the time—Corpus and San Antonio, Victoria and Houston. He played everywhere in Texas, but when I knew Bill he was just playing in Dallas. We played Wassahatchee, Corsicana, and Dallas, a little triangle where the furthest place was around 45 miles away. I met my wife Joy through Bill's ex-wife, Cleta. That was the only blind date I ever went on and I ended up marrying the girl.

He used to go out every weeknight and drink. We used to go down to a place called The Towers in Dallas. There was this bar in there, and all the rounders were there. Monday through Friday night after the poker, Bill would go down there religiously. But he never went on the weekends. So somebody asked him one time why he never went out on the weekends.

"Well," he said, "holidays and weekends are amateur nights. Real drinkers go out during the week."

Shreveport

When I was younger and lived in Shreveport, I had a charge account at Ernest's Supper Club—best food you've ever had in your life—and I was one of the guys running the crap game upstairs at the club. If I didn't have any money I'd just sign my name for the food. They always had a band playing on the dance floor and every time I walked in and they'd stop playing what they had been playing and start up with "I'm Just a Gigolo, Everywhere I Go." Every time I'd walk in the door, I tell you! But I loved to dance and I'd get out there and dance all I could every time I could.

One time, after I'd moved away, I went back down to Shreveport to see Sugar Ray Leonard fight Tommy Hearns, and we went to Earnest's. After dinner we were going out to the fairgrounds to see the fight. We drove 200 miles from Dallas to do this.

And who am I there with? R. D. Matthews, Henry Bowen, and Troy Inman—three of the biggest rounders that ever lived. Henry's the one who did eight years on death row for something he didn't do. But can you imagine going there with those three guys? You talk about a fish out of water, I was really out of water. But I sure felt safe.

You hear about these gangs today? There isn't a one of those guys that this bunch would put up with. They'd look you in the face and shoot you just as soon as spit on the street. I mean they were some tough customers.

The Poker Games in Dallas

These guys I played with in Texas were all great poker players, but they didn't want to just play against each other. You always need producers to feed a game, you know. At one time we had three multi-millionaires playing in the game who would start the game and finish it.

One of them took the cure and joined Gamblers Anonymous, and now he's a bigwig in that organization. And if Hugh Briscoe, who used to have all that land up in Denton, got broke he'd just sell another bit of land so he'd have more poker money. I guess he probably lost $10 million in Dallas. And then there was Ken Smith, who could play but was always on a time schedule, so his money wasn't worth anything. He only had two hours for poker so he tried playing fast. But when Kenny wanted to, he could really play.

But then we got busted, and that was the end of the poker in Dallas. Now they have limit games all over town but it's nothing like it used to be. Somebody asked me recently if there are still games where you can go in and make a killing. Well sure, there are enough poker rooms in California to choke a hog.

Of course, the whole theory of having a cardroom these days is to never spread a big game—you don't want anybody to ever get broke because you want to keep the drop. In this one little town in California there's a cardroom with four or five tables in it but the most they ever get going is two games and $4/$8 is the top limit. This is quite common among many of the smaller clubs.

Bobby Chapman

Every poker game in Dallas or Fort Worth always kept at least one six-pack of Schlitz beer in the refrigerator in case Bobby Chapman showed up. He was the boss gambler in Dallas for years and years, and he used to always bring Nicholas, his big German shepherd, with him to the games. He might not play for three months but if he showed up, he was gonna drink, and he would get bombed after his first beer. I mean, he just couldn't handle alcohol at all. His whole theory of playing poker drunk was, "I'm gonna put enough money on the table that if I beat you one out of five hands, I break you." And he was a dog on most of 'em. When he was sober he played pretty damned good Omaha—but he didn't play very good hold'em.

Bobby was also the one who always put up the money for Art Saling's Omaha game, guaranteed the money and all that. In this particular game, we were playing at the Ramada Inn that Art Saling managed, and three guys who owned pizza places came over to play. This was the first time they'd played with us, and they were horrible players. We were playing a big game with $25/$25/$50 blinds—a really big pot-limit Omaha game—when one memorable pot came up.

I'm on the button, so I'm dealing. The first pizza man calls, another pizza man calls, and here comes Bobby Chapman, and he raises it. Then the third pizza man calls. I'm on the button with 10-9-8-8 with one suit and I decide, "Well, Chapman's liable to be raising with anything and there's a lot of money in the pot. I might be able to win something here." So I reraise the pot about $1,200. First pizza man calls, second pizza man calls, Bobby studies a long time, and then he just flat calls it. I'm thinking, "He's got a big hand, a pair of aces. He's trapping in this hand." Third pizza man calls.

Here comes the flop: A-8-8. I flopped four eights in this pot! First pizza man checks, second pizza man checks, Bobby moves in. Third pizza man folds.

"I think I'll call you, Bobby," I say.

There's over $28,000 in this pot, and he never knew what hit him! This was the one time when Bobby was drunk and really had a hand. You see, a lot of times when he was drunk he'd bet all the way through and on the end he'd say, "Straight flush!" That meant he didn't even have a pair. Of course,

Bobby's such a man, he never said a word, just, "You've got a pretty good hand there, T.J."

I'll tell you what a man he is, what a great guy he actually is. He got involved in a big, big game with a couple of card thieves one summer, and they flat cheated him out of $800,000. Bobby came to us and said, "I know I got cheated out of that money, but I was fool enough to go for it. I lost the money, so I'm paying it." And he paid off every dime he owed right away.

Then he stood good for Art Saling's game and at one time, three people were in over $150,000 in this one game. One of the guys who was in for $150,000 had previously been in with the two other thieves that stole $800,000 from Bobby. When the game was over, this guy didn't have the money to pay off. Even after being cheated out of $800,000, Bobby still paid off the game, made it good.

And you know how this guy was paying him off? $2,000 a month. At that rate, he must have known that he'd never realize the whole $150,000. Hell, he could have had the $150,000 in the bank and made more interest on it than that. But he accepted that, that's what a man he was. Most people who had just been cheated would've said, "Take a long walk on a short pier."

Henry Bowen

Henry Bowen was a real tough guy and a great poker player. In his younger days he was in prison a lot for bank robbery and just from being a super tough guy. And he had little dainty hands—I could never understand how he could be so tough with those little dainty hands.

One Saturday Henry and I went to a rodeo in Tyler, Texas with Johnny Wheeler. Well, I didn't go to the second weekend of the rodeo, but Henry did. Hundreds of witnesses placed him at the rodeo at 11:00 p.m. in Tyler, Texas. At 11:45 p.m., three people—a dope dealer and two others—were murdered by the side of a pool in Oklahoma City. And Henry got charged with the murder.

He was railroaded at the trial because of things he'd done in the past. He was convicted and sat on death row for seven years. Benny Binion, a friend of Henry's, went to bat for him, paying for lawyers and other stuff. Finally, after his story came out on *60 Minutes*, the case was retried and Henry was set free. So Henry had just gotten out of prison after being on death row for seven years and he comes to the poker game run by the Big Texan I told you about in my first book. Henry hated the Big Texan. Now, you can imagine that you might be a little nervous about things if you'd been away for seven years.

He's playing in our game and makes a bet and the Big Texan raises him. Henry's thinking about calling the raise and his hand is shaking a little bit. So the Big Texan says, "How come your hand's shakin', Henry?" to give him the needle while he's thinking about the call. So Henry very quietly turns to the Big Texan and says, "You know, ever since I got out of prison I've been trying to act like a Quaker, you know, tryin' to be nice to everybody. But there's a fine white line, and you've just about stepped over it."

And I mean to tell you, the Big Texan went absolutely white, like a ghost. Henry was not the man you wanted to give a hard time to. The Big Texan went in the front room and watched television for about an hour, scared to death that Henry was going to kill him.

Behavior in Poker Games, Then and Now

Some of these things that people do nowadays in the poker tournaments—acting up and stuff like that—if they weren't killed, they'd have been beaten half to death if they had been playing in Texas in the old days. People wouldn't stand for that kind of behavior back then. There are a lot of hot-blooded players out there today. Sometimes, I get pretty hot inside myself, but I'm not gonna show it. I might mumble once in a while but that's as far as I'm gonna go.

Years ago, Mr. Brooks told us, "If I thought that even one of those other ten players would feel sorry for me, I'd cry every time I had a bad beat, but I know they're all trying to beat me so I'm not gonna show my ignorance."

And I've never forgotten that.

The Owl from Oklahoma

Bobby Baldwin played mostly in Oklahoma but he came down to Dallas and played with us a lot of times. When he was playing poker full-time, he was a great player. Of course, now he's a casino executive and has turned into a pretty tight player. You know how an owl's supposed to be real wise? They called Bobby "The Owl" for just one reason—he was the best hand-reader anywhere.

Bobby Hoff used to say that Bobby was a 15 percent better poker player than any man alive, and that's quite a compliment. If someone is even one percent better, that's something—15 percent better is pretty strong. Even as a kid, Bobby was always a good player. He taught a course in poker one year at Tulsa University. It was an elective class with Bobby Baldwin, professor.

Sailor Roberts

Sailor Roberts was a famous player who did more for down-and-out players than anybody else. If a guy was down on his luck, it was nothing for Sailor to give him a bankroll at any time. Just ask Bobby Hoff, Carl McKelvey, Steve Lott, and all those guys how many people Sailor helped out during his lifetime. He helped Bill Smith a thousand times if he helped him once.

As a player, Sailor could do more with a 4-5 than any man alive. He'd show you that 4-5 three or four times and the next time he raised you'd think he had it again—and he'd have those two eyeballs!

Sailor loved the girls and the parties. One time he went to San Angelo and beat that game out of $85,000 over about a three-month period—and it was a small game, a $5/$10 pot-limit hold'em game. And when he was older he'd leave town with less money than he'd brought with him—that's how much he liked to party with the girls.

I mean, he was a party animal. He just loved three things: golf, poker, and going out with the girls. And boy, they took him for every dime he had. I liked the girls, too, but I wasn't into hookers or anything like that. But Sailor liked any kind of girl. He was a takeout specialist in poker, but the girls were taking him off. They were a little sharper than he was, and he knew it but he didn't care. He just wanted to live life to the fullest.

The Cowboy and the Queen

I was watching a no-limit hold'em game at the Horseshoe a few years back, a $50/$50/$100 blinds game. Cowboy Wolford was playing, and I was sitting behind him. When the dealer dealt the hands out, she exposed a queen. The hand still went, and the queen was used for the burn card. The pot was raised, and there were five callers to Cowboy in the big blind. He has A-Q and he throws it away because a queen is already gone. Now the flop comes A-A-Q!

They started off firing at this pot—Jesse Alto's drunk and bluffing like hell and two players call him. Rusty LePage is drinking and ol' Sam Moon's in there firing, he's stuck. And all the action would have been in front of Cowboy, coming into him. This pot had $60,000 in it if it had a penny. And Alto won it with two sevens—he caught a 7 on the end!

I don't think Cowboy was ever the same after that one. That would've been $60,000 in his pocket. But once that queen gets burned you're playing short-decked, so you can't play the A-Q. I didn't say a word, just got out of my chair and left. I knew that the steam had to be coming out of his ears and everywhere else. I never saw Cowboy play that high again.

Benny Binion

Benny Binion was a piece of work. There are probably a thousand stories that could be told about Benny, but I don't know them all. In his younger days in Dallas, he ran the dice games and other kinds of gambling. In Benny's later years, we used to sit around the Horseshoe and eat breakfast at a big circular table behind the Sombrero Room, and he'd tell us some of the stories about his gambling days back in Texas.

"You never worried about getting broke," he'd say. "If you got broke, you just went out and robbed the bootleggers."

Just push a gun in a bootlegger's face, take his money, and you had a bankroll again. The bootleggers couldn't go to the cops because they were running an illegal business.

When Benny first came to the Horseshoe, he never forgot his old compadres who had gone to jail for a little while here, a little while there. He knew that they wouldn't try to rob him because of his reputation, so he hired them all. When he first started, he had all those thieves working for him. He taught all of them, and they all became great workers—and they were all pro-Benny. That's one of the reasons why the Horseshoe went over so big.

Natey Blank was an old loan shark who had been connected a little bit in the old days. Benny had to take some money from Vegas to Reno and he was worried that Natey knew about it and was going to have him robbed. So he did the right thing: He hired Natey as a bodyguard to go up there with him. Benny was sharp. Just before he died, Natey used to hang out at the Aladdin when they were playing poker there. He was a Las Vegas character, a shylock, for a lot of years.

Benny treated his whole family great, had all of them working in the casino. Of course, there's been a lot of tragedy in that family, you know. First there was Barbara and now Teddy, they're both dead. Barbara had a problem with drugs. We were sitting at breakfast one morning and Benny said, "Fellas, I just let it be known in the whole town that if I hear of one man selling one thing of dope to Barbara, he's a dead man." He tried everything to help her out, but she died from an overdose. I think she was the apple of his eye because he was always talking about her.

Benny helped more people in Vegas than anybody realizes. In the old days all the casinos banked their money on Friday, and they'd keep a certain amount on hand. Well, Benny was always the cash place. If somebody put a big run on one of the casinos, they'd come down and borrow the money from Benny until the banks opened. The ones on the Strip would come downtown and get money from Benny or have the Horseshoe send money out to them so they could have the cash to pay off when somebody put a big hit on them. It didn't happen very often, but he always came through for everybody.

Benny liked to play poker but he wasn't a great player. And of course, it was his idea to get the World Series of Poker started. He wanted to get all the best poker players in the world, put them in one spot, and see who was the best. That was his idea. He always had business in mind, too, so he put them on display, guys like Tommy Abdul, who was a big bookmaker, Billy Davis, and Nick the Greek Dandolos, who was being backed by the Fremont at the time and is famous for having become a millionaire and broke again 77 times. They used to play real high razz over at the Fremont to let people see them playing, and that's one reason why Benny started the World Series. He loved poker.

But above everything else, his real passion was good food. Personally, I never liked his chili but they always called it "Benny Binion's Famous Chili." He had a ranch up in Montana, a big spread. All the beef that they served at the Horseshoe came off his ranch. Jack would run the World Series, but Benny was the one who always made sure the food was right. When Benny was alive, the food was fabulous during the World Series. And he always had some oddball item in the line—buffalo steaks, rattlesnake, bear meat, or this or that.

Every year they had some different thing, and they never had the same buffet twice during the entire World Series. I mean, the main courses were never repeated at any time. This was true all the time that Benny was alive.

There's a little story that came out of Benny's birthday party that involves Ken "Top Hat" Smith. Ken is one of the old-time gamblers around Dallas; he and Doyle have been buddies all their lives and are about the same age.

And he has a top hat from the Ford Theater where Lincoln got shot. He always wore it in the big tournaments, and when he won a hand he'd stand up, doff his hat, and say, "Whatta player, Smith! Whatta player!" Ken was well off money-wise, although his health was poor. You've got to realize that Ken weighed over 400 pounds—he was a huge man.

Just before this birthday party, he went on the Ultra Fast diet and went from 420 pounds down to 247 so that at the time of the party, he weighed less than I did at 252. On this diet all you get to "eat" is some canned powder stuff that you drink in milkshake form. And you have to go to the Baylor clinic for counseling once or twice a week, to be sure that you keep the weight off. Then after you've been on the diet for six or nine months, the people at Ultra Fast give you a three-month hiatus. After that three months is over, they put you on a different plan.

When Benny's birthday tribute came up, Ken was on this hiatus so he could eat some solid food so long as he just stayed away from fattening foods. He and his wife, Elaine, and my wife Joy and I went together to the party. The eats were fantastic: The fella who used to be the head chef at the Horseshoe had arranged the menu and supervised all the food.

Well, Ken took a plate of food that you couldn't believe—it looked like a mountain on top of one of those thin paper plates. And he ate every bit of it.

Then they broke out Benny's birthday cake. It was a tall, three-tiered thing that was bigger than a wedding cake by a long shot. And Ken Smith went up there to get a slice of it—he asked for a big slice because he loves sweets and all that frosting and stuff—and he ate that piece of cake like it was nothing.

You know how the frosting sticks to paper plates? He was running his finger around the edge to pick up the icing so he could lick it off his finger. I told Joy right then, "You can forget about the diet. He's never goin' back to it again."

Doyle Takes a Dinner Break

Several years ago during Amarillo Slim's tournament at Caesars, Doyle Brunson and I were playing at the same table. During the dinner break he went off and played some high-limit hold'em. When we resumed playing the tournament after the break, he leaned back in his chair and said, "If I can win the $51,000 they're giving away for first place, I'll only be $14,000 loser for the dinner break!"

GLOSSARY
OF
POKER TERMS

GLOSSARY OF POKER TERMS

Backdoor a flush/straight

Make a hand that you were not originally drawing to by catching favorable cards on later streets. "In Omaha there are so many **backdoor** possibilities that are unseen. A lot of times, you'll raise the pot with a hand like A-A-10-9 and you'll wind up winning the pot with a straight, not the aces."

Backup

A card that provides you with an extra out. "If you have a drawing hand, you should have a **backup** to your draw, a secondary draw. You always want an extra low card in Omaha high-low to back-up your ace-deuce."

Beat into the pot

When an opponent bets an inferior hand, and you gladly—and quickly—push your chips into the pot. "When three clubs came on the flop, Slim moved in. I **beat him into the pot** with my flush—he had a 10-high flush, mine was higher."

Behind

Describes a table position in which other players will have to act before you do. "So long as you're sitting **behind** the other players, you have the advantage of position."

Big flop

A flop that greatly enhances the strength of your hand. "I caught a **big flop** that gave me the nut flush, a wheel, and a set."

Big rundown

A hand in which your high cards are connected. See **rundown**. "When the flop came Q-10-9, my **big rundown** connected perfectly with it, giving me a king-high straight."

Boss hand

The best possible high hand. "When you have the **boss** high **hand**, you should bet it as aggressively as possible, especially if you think two low hands are out there."

Bully

To play aggressively. "When I have a big stack in a tournament, I like being able to **bully** the entire table."

Change gears

To adjust your style of play from fast to slow, from loose to tight, from raising to calling, and so on. "When the cards quit coming his way, Will didn't **change gears**; instead, he kept on playing fast and lost his whole bankroll."

Cold call

To call a raise without having put an initial bet into the pot. "Bonetti raised, Hellmuth reraised, and I **cold called**."

Come over the top

To raise or reraise. "I raised it $2,000 and Sexton **came over the top** of me with $7,000."

Commit fully/fully commit

To put in as many chips as necessary to play your hand to the river, even if they are your case chips. "If I think the odds are in my favor, I will **fully commit**."

Counterfeited

Describes the situation in which your nut low hand gets demoted by cards on the board that duplicate your hole cards. "You should always have a third low card to help out against getting **counterfeited**."

Dangler

A fourth card that doesn't fit in with your other three cards. "K-Q-J-6, three high cards with a **dangler**—who the hell wants to play that kind of hand? That **dangler** can put you in a world of misery."

Decision hand

A hand that requires you to make a value judgment. "The great hands and the trash hands play themselves. It is the **decision hands** that will determine your profit at the end of the session, the day, the year. Playing all of the marginal, in-between hands with great ability is what separates winners from losers."

Flat call

To call a bet without raising. "When he bet in to me, I just **flat called** to keep the players behind me from folding."

Flop to it

To flop cards that enhance the value of your hand. "If you don't **flop to it**, you can get away from the hand."

Get away from it

To fold, usually when what appeared to be a premium hand took an unfavorable flop that negated its potential. "If you don't flop to the low, **get away from it**."

Get the right price

To have pot odds that are favorable enough for you to justify calling a bet or a raise with a drawing hand. "Since I was **getting the right price**, I called the bet with a wraparound."

Get full value

To bet, raise, and reraise in order to increase the size of the pot that you stand to win. "By raising on every round, I was able to get **full value** when my hand held up at the river."

Get there

To make your hand. "When you **get there**, you might be able to start maximizing your bets."

Give him

To attribute a hand to your opponent(s). "When the flop comes with a pair and your opponent raises, what are you going to **give him**? A straight draw?"

Gypsy in

To enter the pot for the same price as the big blind. "I wanted to play my A-A-2-3 deceptively in the Omaha high-low tournament, so I decided to just **gypsy in**."

High wrap

Cards that will complete a straight, no matter what high card comes on the turn or river. "When the board came with a 5-9-10, I flopped the **high wrap** with my K-Q-J-10."

Implied odds

The future bets that can potentially be won compared to the cost of your bet. "T.J. didn't have the best hand on the pot-limit flop, but his **implied odds** were so great, he bet the size of the pot.

Inside wrap

Cards with ranks between the highest and lowest cards on the flop. "If the flop comes with A-10-4 and you have K-Q-J-9 in your hand, you have an **inside wrap**."

Isolate

To raise or reraise in order to limit the action to yourself and one opponent. "Suppose you have **isolated** an opponent in pot-limit Omaha and you know that he has aces. If you flop a wraparound, you might continue with the hand since you have only one person to beat."

Jammed pot

A pot that has been raised the maximum number of times. "You should pass with a weak hand if the pot has been **jammed** before it gets to you."

Key card

The one card that will make your hand a winner. "I knew that I needed to catch a deuce, the **key card** to my wheel draw."

Lay down a hand

To fold. "Many times, you can put enough pressure on the pot to blow everybody away and sometimes even get the raiser to **lay down** his hand."

Limp in

To enter the pot by just calling rather than raising. "In Omaha high-low you might want to **limp in** from up- front with a premium low hand, such as A-2-4-5."

Limpers

Players who enter the pot for the minimum bet. "With three **limpers** in the pot, I thought that my pair of kings probably was the best hand."

Little rundown

A hand in which your small cards are connected. See **rundown**. "You might call in late position with a **little rundown** in pot-limit Omaha if you think that all your opponents are holding high cards."

Live cards

Cards that you need to improve your hand and which probably are still available to you. "When three players who I knew to be big-pair players entered the pot in front of me, I thought my middle connectors might still be **live** so I decided to play the hand."

Live one

A loose, inexperienced, or bad player. "Very seldom do you get a **live one**, a person who can't play at all, in the big games but it does happen sometimes."

Long call

To think a long time before calling a bet. "When you make a **long call**, your opponents usually figure that you're weak and will come after you in a later betting round."

Low wrap

The cards in your hand will make a low straight if one other connecting low cards hits the board. "When the 3-6-7 hit the board, I had the **low wrap** with my A-2-4-8."

Maine to Spain

Describes a hand that will allow to make your hand by catching any card on either end of the flop cards, or one of your own cards. "Suppose the flops comes J-10-2 and you have K-Q-9-8—we call it **Maine to Spain**—that's a big, *big* hand."

Make a move

To attempt a bluff. "When the board paired sixes, Max **made a move** at the pot. I thought he was bluffing but I had nothing to call him with."

Middle buster

An inside straight draw. "If the flop comes A-10-4 and you have the Q-J-10-8, you're not going to draw to the **middle buster**. Try to catch the king."

Multiway draw

A draw to a hand that has multiple possibilities for winning. "My A-2-3-5 suited gave me a **multiway draw** to the nut low as well as a draw to the nut flush on the flop."

Nit and Supernit

A very tight player and a super-tight player. "A **nit** is a person who plays tight and takes no chances. The **supernit** will drive from one county to the other, win one pot, quit the game, and drive home."

Nut draw

A draw to the best possible hand. "When two clubs come on the board and you have the A♣ 4♣, you have the **nut** flush **draw**."

Nuts

The best hand possible at the moment. "Remember that you can flop the **nuts** and lose it on the turn. That's why in pot-limit Omaha you sometimes lay down the nuts on the flop against any action."

Nutted up

Describes someone who is playing very tight. "Jackson was so **nutted up** at the final table, I stole pot after pot from him."

Out

A card that completes your hand. "Always try to have an extra **out**, a third low card to go with your ace, when you're drawing for the low end."

Outside wrap

Three of your downcards combine with two cards on the board—the holecards "wrapping" on both ends of the five-card sequence—to form a straight. "When the flop came J-10-4, Greg had an **outside wrap** with his K-Q-9-8 holecards."

Overpair

A pair that is higher than the highest card showing on the board. "I flopped an **overpair**, but folded against the action in front of me."

Pay off

To call an opponent's bet at the river even though you think that he might have the best hand. "When the board paired at the river and he bet, I decided to **pay him off** because I didn't think that he had made trips."

Peddling the nuts

Drawing to, playing, and betting the nut hand. "Remember that in Omaha, players are **peddling the nuts** 90 percent of the time. They may not be peddling them in a heads-up situation, but in any multiway pot, somebody's drawing at the nuts if he doesn't already have it."

Perfects

Premium low cards, ace through 5. "Tom looked down at four **perfects** in the blind, A-2-4-5."

Piece of cheese

A hand that is a loser. "If you raise and get reraised, your trip threes are probably a **piece of cheese**, so be very careful when you flop bottom set."

Play back

To respond to an opponent's bet by either raising or reraising. "If a tight opponent **plays back** at you, you know he probably has the nuts."

Play from behind

To check when you have a big hand, with the intent of check-raising. "I knew that Kevin usually **played from behind** when he had a big hand, so when he checked, so did I."

Play fast

To bet a drawing hand aggressively in order to get full value for it if you make it. "Many players **play fast** in the early rounds of rebuy tournaments to try to build their stacks."

Play slow

To wait and see what develops before pushing a hand. "When you make the nut straight on the flop and there's a chance that the flush draw or a set is out, why not **play** your hand **slow** to start with?"

Play with

To stay in the hand by betting, calling, raising, or reraising. "You should realize that in Omaha high-low, you're going to get **played with** most of the time because it's a limit-structure game, meaning that there usually are a lot of players in every pot."

Pure

Certain. "In limit poker it is almost 90 percent **pure** that anyone who has called a bet on the flop will also call a raise on the flop."

Put on the heat

To pressure your opponents with aggressive betting strategies to get the most value from your hand. "You might consider **putting on the heat** when your opponent is slightly conservative or when he has a short stack against your big stack."

Put an opponent on a hand

To assign a value to your opponent's hand based upon the information available to you. "Using my instincts and the way he had played the hand, I **put** Stanley **on** the nut low."

Rag

A board card that doesn't help you and appears not to have helped anyone else, either. Also called a **blank**. "The flop came with A-2-3 and then a **rag**, the 9♠, hit on the turn."

Rag off

When the river card doesn't help you. "Then it **ragged off** on the end, and he was a gone goose for all his money."

Rainbow

Describes a flop with three different suits. "I liked my straight draw when the flop came **rainbow** and nobody could have a flush draw against me."

Read the board

To understand the value of your hand in relation to the community cards. "If you **read the board** correctly, you often can tell by the action that you might get a fourth of the pot with your A-2."

Rock

A very conservative player who always waits for premium cards before he plays a hand. "Smith was playing like a **rock** so when she bet in to me, I knew she had me beat."

Run over

To play aggressively in an attempt to control the other players. "If they're not trying to stop you from being a bully, then keep **running over** them until they do."

Rundown hand

A hand in which your cards are connected. "If it's a small **rundown hand** such as 6-5-4-3, being suited only comes into play when you're heads up."

Runner-runner

Cards on the turn and river that make a hand a winner. "As it turns out, you had a suited K-J, caught **runner-runner** to make a flush, and broke me!"

Showdown

The situation that arises when two or more players remain after all betting is completed on the river and the cards are turned over to determine the winner. "If everyone checks to you at the river and you couldn't win in a **showdown**, why bet if you know that you will get called?"

Scoop the pot

To win both the high and low ends of a pot in a split game. "The whole idea of Omaha high-low is to play hands that you can **scoop the pot** with."

Scooper

A hand that wins the whole pot. "When a third low card failed to come at the river, I had a **scooper**."

Slowplay

To intentionally not bet a strong hand for maximum value in order to trap your opponents. "When pot-limit hold'em players move to pot-limit Omaha, they often make the mistake of using **slowplay** tactics to try to trap people. But you can't give free cards in Omaha. You don't **slowplay**; you play very straightforwardly. If you have it, you bet it."

Spaces

A gap between cards in a straight draw. "When I saw the flop, I was one happy camper when it filled the **spaces** in my A-Q-10-8 holecards."

Stand a raise

To call a raise. "I recently **stood a raise** in a cash game with 9-9-8-7. The board came 7-6-2, no suits. A guy led off with a decent bet, and I called him with my overpair and straight draw."

Stiffed in

To play a blind hand in an unraised pot. "The only time you might play middle connectors in Omaha high-low is when you're in the big blind and get **stiffed in**."

Smooth-call

To call a bet without raising. "If someone bets into you, you might **smooth-call** with this type of hand since you have an extra out."

Take off a card

To call a bet on the flop. "I decided to **take off a card** and see what the turn would bring."

Takeoff hand

A hand that has the potential of beating a better starting hand because it is live. "In four-way action, I figured that my middle connectors might turn into a **takeoff hand**."

Take an opponent off a hand

To beat a superior starting hand. "Any of those types of hands—ones in which you have three rundown cards with a pair—will **take the aces right off** a lot of times."

There (get there)

To make a hand. "Sometimes when you don't **get there** till the river, you're sweating bullets all the way."

Underbet

A bet in no-limit or pot-limit that is considerably smaller than the maximum bet allowed. "You don't make a small bet to try to pick up a big pot. The **underbet** is a tip-off that you have a big hand."

Underpair

A pair that is lower than a pair showing on the board. "Why would you ever want to call with an **underpair**?"

Wake up with a hand

To be dealt a hand with winning potential. "Just because a player is a maniac doesn't mean that he can't **wake up with a hand**. Over the long haul, everybody gets the same number of good hands and bad hands."

Where you're at

The value of your hand in relation to the other players' hands. "Your opponent may not know for sure **where you're at** in the hand when you have played it in a deceptive way."

World's fair

A big hand. "Suppose the flop comes 8-8-4, no suits. You know you're up against either nothing or the **world's fair**."

Wraparound or Wrap

A hand in which the connectors wrap perfectly around the flop cards, giving you multiple ways to make a straight. "Suppose the flop comes 10-7-2 and you have J-9-8-6 in your hand. That's a complete **wrap**—you can catch a card on either end or in the middle and make your hand."

GREAT CARDOZA POKER BOOKS
ADD THESE TO YOUR LIBRARY - ORDER NOW!

DANIEL NEGREANU'S POWER HOLD'EM STRATEGY *by Daniel Negreanu.* This power-packed book on beating no-limit hold'em is one of the three most influential poker books ever written. Negreanu headlines a collection of young great players—Todd Brunson, David Williams. Eric Lindgren, Evelyn Ng and Paul Wasicka—who share their insider professional moves and winning secrets. You'll learn about short-handed and heads-up play, high-limit cash games, a powerful beginner's strategy to neutralize professional players, and how to mix up your play and bluff and win big pots. The centerpiece, however, is Negreanu's powerful and revolutionary small ball strategy. You'll learn how to play hold'em with cards you never would have played before—and with fantastic results. The preflop, flop, turn and river will never look the same again. A must-have! 500 pages, $34.95.

POKER WIZARDS *by Warwick Dunnett.* In the tradition of Super System, an exclusive collection of champions and superstars have been brought together to share their strategies, insights, and tactics for winning big money at poker, specifically no-limit hold'em tournaments. This is priceless advice from players who individually have each made millions of dollars in tournaments, and collectively, have won more than 20 WSOP bracelets, two WSOP main events, 100 major tournaments and $50 million in tournament winnings! Featuring Daniel Negreanu, Dan Harrington, Marcel Luske, Kathy Liebert, Mike Sexton, Mel Judah, Marc Salem, T.J Cloutier and Chris "Jesus" Ferguson. This must-read book is a goldmine for all serious players, aspiring pros, and future champions! 352 pgs, $19.95.

HOLD'EM WISDOM FOR ALL PLAYERS *By Daniel Negreanu.* Superstar poker player Daniel Negreanu provides 50 easy-to-read and right-to-the-point hold'em strategy nuggets that will immediately make you a better player at cash games and tournaments. His wit and wisdom makes for great reading; even better, it makes for killer winning advice. Conversational, straightforward, and educational, this book covers topics as diverse as the top 10 rookie mistakes to bullying bullies and exploiting your table image. 176 pages, $14.95.

OMAHA HIGH-LOW: How to Win at the Lower Limits *by Shane Smith.* Practical advice specifically targeted for the popular low-limit games you play every day in casinos and online will have you making money, and show you how to avoid losing situations and cards that can cost you a bundle—the dreaded second-nut draws, trap hands, and two-way second-best action. Smith's proven strategies are spiced with plenty of wit and wisdom. You'll learn the basics of play against the typical opponents you'll face in low-limit games—the no-fold'em players and the rocks—and get winning tactics, illustrated hands, and tournament tips guaranteed to improve your game. 144 pages, $12.95.

TOURNAMENT TIPS FROM THE POKER PROS *by Shane Smith.* Essential advice from poker theorists, authors, and tournament winners on the best strategies for winning the big prizes at low-limit rebuy tournaments. Learn proven strategies for each of the four stages of play—opening, middle, late and final—how to avoid 26 potential traps, advice on rebuys, aggressive play, clock-watching, inside moves, top 20 tips for winning tournaments, more. Advice from Brunson, McEvoy, Cloutier, Caro, Malmuth, others. 160 pages, $14.95.

NO-LIMIT TEXAS HOLD 'EM *by Brad Daugherty & Tom McEvoy.* New Edition! Twelve power-packed courses cover the full gamut of winning no-limit hold'em tournaments! Two World Champions of Poker, Brad Daugherty and Tom McEvoy, the "Champion of Champions," give you unmatched practical advice on how to beat the low buy-in tournaments played everywhere. Includes more than 70 play-by-play examples using all the key hand categories. Learn how to make the right decision from two proven winners. 224 pages, $19.95.

GREAT CARDOZA POKER BOOKS
ADD THESE TO YOUR LIBRARY - ORDER NOW!

THE POKER TOURNAMENT FORMULA *by Arnold Snyder.* Start making money now in fast no-limit hold'em tournaments with these radical and never-before-published concepts and secrets for beating tournaments. You'll learn why cards don't matter as much as the dynamics of a tournament—your position, the size of your chip stack, who your opponents are, and above all, the structure. Poker tournaments offer one of the richest opportunities to come along in decades. Every so often, a book comes along that changes the way players attack a game and provides them with a big advantage over opponents. Gambling legend Arnold Snyder has written such a book. 368 pages, $19.95.

POKER TOURNAMENT FORMULA 2: Advanced Strategies for Big Money Tournaments *by Arnold Snyder.* Probably the greatest tournament poker book ever written, and the most controversial in the last decade, Snyder's revolutionary work debunks commonly (and falsely) held beliefs. Snyder reveals the power of chip utility—the real secret behind winning tournaments—and covers utility ranks, tournament structures, small- and long-ball strategies, patience factors, the impact of structures, crushing the Harringbots and other player types, tournament phases, and much more. Includes big sections on Tools, Strategies, and Tournament Phases. A must buy! 496 pages, $24.95.

CRASH COURSE IN BEATING TEXAS HOLD'EM *by Avery Cardoza.* Perfect for beginning and somewhat experienced players who want to jump right in on the action and play cash games, local tournaments, online poker, and the big televised tournaments where millions of dollars can be made. Both limit and no-limit hold'em games are covered along with the essential strategies needed to play profitably on the preflop, flop, turn, and river. The good news is that you don't need to memorize hands or be burdened by math to be a winner—just play by the no-nonsense basic principles outlined here. 208 pages, $14.95

POKER TALK: Learn How to Talk Poker Like a Pro *by Avery Cardoza.* This fascinating and fabulous collection of colorful poker words, phrases, and poker-speak features more than 2,000 definitions. No longer is it enough to know how to walk the walk in poker, you need to know how to talk the talk! Learn what it means to go all in on a rainbow flop with pocket rockets and get it cracked by cowboys, put a bad beat on a calling station, and go over the top of a producer fishing with a gutshot to win a big dime. You'll soon have those railbirds wondering what *you* are talking about. 304 pages, $9.95.

OMAHA HIGH-LOW: Play to Win with the Odds *by Bill Boston.* Selecting the right hands to play is the most important decision to make in Omaha. This is the *only* book that shows you the chances that every one of the 5,278 Omaha high-low hands has of winning the high end of the pot, the low end of it, and how often it is expected to scoop all the chips. You get all the vital tools needed to make critical preflop decisions based on the results of more than 500 million computerized hand simulations. You'll learn the 100 most profitable starting cards, trap hands to avoid, 49 worst hands, 30 ace-less hands you can play for profit, and the three bandit cards you must know to avoid losing hands. 248 pages, $19.95.

HOW TO BEAT SIT-AND-GO POKER TOURNAMENTS by Neil Timothy. There is a lot of dead money up for grabs in the lower limit sit-and-gos and Neil Timothy shows you how to go and get it. The author, a professional player, shows you how to reach the last six places of lower limit sit-and-go tournaments four out of five times and then how to get in the money 25-35 percent of the time using his powerful, proven strategies. This book can turn a losing sit-and-go player into a winner, and a winner into a bigger winner. Also effective for the early and middle stages of one-table satellites.176 pages, $14.95.

Order now at 1-800-577-WINS or go online to: www.cardozabooks.com

DOYLE BRUNSON'S EXCITING BOOKS
ADD THESE TO YOUR COLLECTION - ORDER NOW!

SUPER SYSTEM *by Doyle Brunson*. This classic book is considered by the pros to be the best book ever written on poker! Jam-packed with advanced strategies, theories, tactics and money-making techniques, no serious poker player can afford to be without this hard-hitting information. Includes fifty pages of the most precise poker statistics ever published. Features chapters written by poker's biggest superstars, such as Dave Sklansky, Mike Caro, Chip Reese, Joey Hawthorne, Bobby Baldwin, and Doyle. Essential strategies, advanced play, and no-nonsense winning advice on making money at 7-card stud (razz, high-low split, cards speak, and declare), draw poker, lowball, and hold'em (limit and no-limit).This is a must-read for any serious poker player. 628 pages, $29.95.

SUPER SYSTEM 2 *by Doyle Brunson*. SS2 expands upon the original with more games and professional secrets from the best in the world. New revision includes Phil Hellmuth Jr. along with superstar contributors Daniel Negreanu, winner of multiple WSOP gold bracelets and 2004 Poker Player of the Year; Lyle Berman, 3-time WSOP gold bracelet winner, founder of the World Poker Tour, and super-high stakes cash player; Bobby Baldwin, 1978 World Champion; Johnny Chan, 2-time World Champion and 10-time WSOP bracelet winner; Mike Caro, poker's greatest researcher, theorist, and instructor; Jennifer Harman, the world's top female player and one of ten best overall; Todd Brunson, winner of more than 20 tournaments; and Crandell Addington, no-limit hold'em legend. 704 pgs, $29.95.

CARO'S GUIDE TO DOYLE BRUNSON'S SUPER SYSTEM *by Mike Caro*. Working with World Champion Doyle Brunson, the legendary Mike Caro has created a fresh look to the "Bible" of all poker books, adding new and personal insights that help you understand the original work. Caro breaks 36 concepts into either "Analysis, Commentary, Concept, Mission, Play-By-Play, Psychology, Statistics, Story, or Strategy. Lots of illustrations and winning concepts give even more value to this great work. 86 pages, 8 1/2 x 11, $19.95.

ACCORDING TO DOYLE *by Doyle Brunson*. Learn what it takes to be a great poker player by climbing inside the mind of poker's most famous champion. Fascinating anecdotes and adventures from Doyle's early career playing poker in roadhouses are interspersed with lessons from the champion who has made more money at poker than anyone else in history. Learn what makes a great player tick, how he approaches the game, and receive candid, powerful advice from the legend himself. 208 pages, $14.95.

MY 50 MOST MEMORABLE HANDS *by Doyle Brunson*. This instant classic relives the most incredible hands by the greatest poker player of all time. Great players, legends, and poker's most momentous events march in and out of fifty years of unforgettable hands. Sit side-by-side with Doyle as he replays the excitement and life-changing moments of the most thrilling and crucial hands in the history of poker: from his early games as a rounder in the rough-and-tumble "Wild West" years—where a man was more likely to get shot as he was to get a straight flush—to the nail-biting excitement of his two world championship titles. Relive million dollar hands and the high stakes tension of sidestepping police, hijackers and murderers. A thrilling collection of stories and sage poker advice. 168 pages, $14.95.

ONLINE POKER *by Doyle Brunson*. Ten compelling chapters show you how to get started, explain the safety features which lets you play worry-free, and lets you in on the strategies that Doyle himself uses to beat players in cyberspace. Poker is poker, as Doyle explains, but there are also strategies that only apply to the online version, where the players are weaker!—and Doyle reveals them all in this book.192 pages, illustrations, $14.95.

BOBBY BALDWIN'S WINNING POKER SECRETS *by Mike Caro with Bobby Baldwin*. The fascinating account of 1978 World Champion Bobby Baldwin's early career playing poker against other legends is packed with valuable insights. Covers the common mistakes average players make at seven poker variations and the dynamic winning concepts needed for success. Endorsed by superstars Doyle Brunson and Amarillo Slim. 208 pages, $14.95.

MIKE CARO'S EXCITING WORK
POWERFUL BOOKS YOU <u>MUST</u> HAVE

CARO'S MOST PROFITABLE HOLD'EM ADVICE *by Mike Caro.* When Mike Caro writes a book on winning, all poker players take notice. And they should: The "Mad Genius of Poker" has influenced just about every professional player and world champion alive. You'll journey far beyond the traditional tactical tools offered in most poker books and for the first time, have access to the entire missing arsenal of strategies left out of everything you've ever seen or experienced. Caro's first major work in two decades is packed with hundreds of powerful ideas, concepts, and strategies, many of which will be new to you—they have never been made available to the general public. This book represents Caro's lifelong research into beating the game of hold em. 408 pages, $24.95

MASTERING HOLD'EM AND OMAHA *by Mike Caro and Mike Cappelletti.* Learn the professional secrets to mastering the two most popular games of big-money poker: hold'em and Omaha. This is a thinking player's book, packed with ideas, with the focus is on making you a winning player. You'll learn everything from the strategies for play on the preflop, flop, turn and river, to image control and taking advantage of players stuck in losing patterns. You'll also learn how to create consistent winning patterns, use perception to gain an edge, avoid common errors, go after and win default pots, recognize and use the various types of raises, play marginal hands for profit, the importance of being loved or feared, and Cappelletti's unique point count system for Omaha. 328 pages, $19.95.

CARO'S BOOK OF POKER TELLS *by Mike Caro.* One of the ten greatest books written on poker, this must-have book should be in every player's library. If you're serious about winning, you'll realize that most of the profit comes from being able to read your opponents. Caro reveals the the secrets of interpreting *tells*—physical reactions that reveal information about a player's cards—such as shrugs, sighs, shaky hands, eye contact, and many more. Learn when opponents are bluffing, when they aren't and why—based solely on their mannerisms. Over 170 photos of players in action and play-by-play examples show the actual tells. These powerful ideas will give you the decisive edge. 320 pages, $24.95.

CARO'S FUNDAMENTAL SECRETS OF WINNING POKER *by Mike Caro.* Learn the essential strategies, concepts, and plays that comprise the very foundation of winning poker play. Learn to win more from weak players, equalize stronger players, bluff a bluffer, win big pots, where to sit against weak players, and the six factors of strategic table image. Includes selected tips on hold 'em, 7 stud, draw, lowball, tournaments, more. 160 pages, $12.95.

CARO'S PROFESSIONAL POKER REPORTS

Each of these three powerful insider poker reports is centered around a daily mission, with the goal of adding one weapon per day to your arsenal. Theoretical concepts and practical situations are mixed together for fast in-depth learning. For serious players.

11 DAYS TO 7-STUD SUCCESS. Bluffing, playing and defending pairs, different strategies for the different streets, analyzing situations—lots of information within. One advantage is gained each day. A quick and powerful method to 7-stud winnings. Essential. Signed, numbered. $19.95.

12 DAYS TO HOLD'EM SUCCESS. Positional thinking, playing and defending against mistakes, small pairs, flop situations, playing the river, are just some sample lessons. Guaranteed to make you a better player. Very popular. Signed, numbered. $19.95.

PROFESSIONAL 7-STUD REPORT. When to call, pass, and raise, playing starting hands, aggressive play, 4th and 5th street concepts, lots more. Tells how to read an opponent's starting hand, plus sophisticated advanced strategies. Important revision for serious players. Signed, numbered. $19.95.

THE CHAMPIONSHIP SERIES
POWERFUL INFORMATION YOU <u>MUST</u> HAVE

CHAMPIONSHIP NO-LIMIT & POT-LIMIT HOLD'EM *by T. J. Cloutier & Tom McEvoy.* New edition! The bible for winning pot-limit and no-limit hold'em gives you the answers to your most important questions: How do you get inside your opponents' heads and learn how to beat them at their own game? How can you tell how much to bet, raise, and reraise in no-limit hold'em? When can you bluff? How do you set up your opponents in pot-limit hold'em so that you can win a monster pot? What are the best strategies for winning no-limit and pot-limit tournaments, satellites, and supersatellites? Rock-solid and inspired advice you can bank on from two of the most recognizable figures in poker. 304 pages, $19.95.

CHAMPIONSHIP HOLD'EM *by T. J. Cloutier & Tom McEvoy.* New edition! Hard-hitting hold'em the way it's played *today* in both limit cash games and tournaments. Get killer advice on how to win more money in rammin'-jammin' games, kill-pot, jackpot, shorthanded, and full table cash games. You'll learn the thinking process for preflop, flop, turn, and river play with specific suggestions for what to do when good or bad things happen. Includes play-by-play analyses, advice on how to maximize profits against rocks in tight games, weaklings in loose games, experts in solid games, plus tournament strategies for small buy-in, big buy-in, rebuy, satellite and big-field major tournaments. Wow! 392 pages, $19.95.

CHAMPIONSHIP OMAHA (Omaha High-Low, Pot-limit Omaha, Limit High Omaha) *by Tom McEvoy & T.J. Cloutier.* New edition! Clearly-written strategies and powerful advice from Cloutier and McEvoy who have won four World Series of Poker Omaha titles. You'll learn how to beat low-limit and high-stakes games, play against loose and tight opponents, and the differing strategies for rebuy and freezeout tournaments. Learn the best starting hands, when slowplaying a big hand is dangerous, what danglers are (and why winners don't play them), why you sometimes fold the nuts on the flop and would be correct in doing so, and overall, how you can win a lot of money at Omaha! 272 pages, illustrations, $19.95.

CHAMPIONSHIP HOLD'EM TOURNAMENT HANDS *by T. J. Cloutier & Tom McEvoy.* An absolute must for hold'em tournament players, two legends show you how to become a winning tournament player at both limit and no-limit hold'em games. Get inside the authors' heads as they think their way through the correct strategy at 57 limit and no-limit starting hands. Cloutier & McEvoy show you how to use skill and intuition to play strategic hands for maximum profit in real tournament scenarios and how 45 key hands were played by champions in turnaround situations at the WSOP. Gain tremendous insights into how tournament poker is played at the highest levels. 368 pages, $29.95.

CHAMPIONSHIP HOLD'EM SATELLITE STRATEGY *by World Champions Brad Dougherty & Tom McEvoy.* Every year satellite players win their way into the $10,000 WSOP buy-in and emerge as millionaires or champions. You can too! Learn the specific, proven strategies for winning almost any satellite from two world champions. Covers the ten ways to win a seat at the WSOP, how to win limit hold'em and no-limit hold'em satellites, one-table satellites, online satellites, and the final table of super satellites. Includes a special chapter on no-limit hold'em satellites! 320 pages, $29.95.

HOW TO WIN THE CHAMPIONSHIP: Hold'em Strategies for the Final Table, *by T.J. Cloutier.* If you're hungry to win a championship, this is the book that will pave the way! T.J. Cloutier, the greatest tournament poker player ever—he has won 60 major tournament titles and appeared at 39 final tables at the WSOP, both more than any other player in the history of poker—shows how to get to the final table where the big money is made and then how to win it all. You'll learn how to build up enough chips to make it through the early and middle rounds and then how to employ T.J.'s own strategies to outmaneuver opponents at the final table and win championships. You'll learn how to adjust your play depending upon stack sizes, antes/blinds, table position, opponents styles, chip counts, and the specific strategies for six-handed, three handed, and heads-up play. 288 pages, $29.95.

POWERFUL WINNING POKER SIMULATIONS
A MUST FOR SERIOUS PLAYERS WITH A COMPUTER!
IBM compatible CD ROM Win 95, 98, 2000, NT, ME, XP

These incredible full color poker simulations are the best method to improve your game. Computer opponents play like real players. All games let you set the limits and rake and have fully programmable players, plus stat tracking, and Hand Analyzer for starting hands. MIke Caro, the world's foremost poker theoretician says, "Amazing... a steal for under $500... get it, it's great." Includes free phone support. "Smart Advisor" gives expert advice for every play!

1. TURBO TEXAS HOLD'EM FOR WINDOWS - $59.95. Choose which players, and how many (2-10) you want to play, create loose/tight games, and control check-raising, bluffing, position, sensitivity to pot odds, and more! Also, instant replay, pop-up odds, Professional Advisor keeps track of play statistics. Free bonus: Hold'em Hand Analyzer analyzes all 169 pocket hands in detail and their win rates under any conditions you set. Caro says this "hold'em software is the most powerful ever created." Great product!

2. TURBO SEVEN-CARD STUD FOR WINDOWS - $59.95. Create any conditions of play; choose number of players (2-8), bet amounts, fixed or spread limit, bring-in method, tight/loose conditions, position, reaction to board, number of dead cards, and stack deck to create special conditions. Features instant replay. Terrific stat reporting includes analysis of starting cards, 3-D bar charts, and graphs. Play interactively and run high speed simulation to test strategies. Hand Analyzer analyzes starting hands in detail. Wow!

3. TURBO OMAHA HIGH-LOW SPLIT FOR WINDOWS - $59.95. Specify any playing conditions; betting limits, number of raises, blind structures, button position, aggressiveness/passiveness of opponents, number of players (2-10), types of hands dealt, blinds, position, board reaction, and specify flop, turn, and river cards! Choose opponents and use provided point count or create your own. Statistical reporting, instant replay, pop-up odds high speed simulation to test strategies, amazing Hand Analyzer, and much more!

4. TURBO OMAHA HIGH FOR WINDOWS - $59.95. Same features as above, but tailored for Omaha High only. Caro says program is "an electrifying research tool...it can clearly be worth thousands of dollars to any serious player. A must for Omaha High players.

5. TURBO 7 STUD 8 OR BETTER - $59.95. Brand new with all the features you expect from the Wilson Turbo products: the latest artificial intelligence, instant advice and exact odds, play versus 2-7 opponents, enhanced data charts that can be exported or printed, the ability to fold out of turn and immediately go to the next hand, ability to peek at opponents hand, optional warning mode that warns you if a play disagrees with the advisor, and automatic mode that runs up to 50 tests unattended. Tough computer players vary their styles for a great game.

6. TOURNAMENT TEXAS HOLD'EM - $39.95

Set-up for tournament practice and play, this realistic simulation pits you against celebrity look-alikes. Tons of options let you control tournament size with 10 to 300 entrants, select limits, ante, rake, blind structures, freezeouts, number of rebuys and competition level of opponents. Pop-up status report shows how you're doing vs. the competition. Save tournaments in progress to play again later. Additional feature allows quick folds on finished hands.

Order now at 1-800-577-WINS or go online to: www.cardozabooks.com